David Wood was educated at the University of Nottingham. In 1970 he went as SRC/NATO Fellow to the Center for Cognitive Studies at Harvard University where he began working with Jerome Bruner. He returned to Nottingham in 1972 as Lecturer in Psychology and in 1977–8 worked in the Department of Educational Studies at the University of Oxford on a Fellowship funded jointly by the Nuffield Foundation and by SSRC. His published work ranges from contributions to the development of robots to studies of teaching methods. One aspect of his current research, based centrally on the work with the Oxford Preschool Research Group, concerns the work of teachers with deaf children.

Linnet McMahon read sociology and social psychology at the Universities of Exeter and Birmingham, and first became interested in under-fives while studying child development and education in California. She later taught at a New York liberal arts college, and also made a study of Swiss pre-schools. She has herself been involved in starting a preschool playgroup, and now tutors playgroup courses, as well as working on the research committee of the PPA. The Joseph Rowntree Memorial Trust supports a current project to produce practical resource materials for playgroup courses, based on the work of the Oxford Preschool Research Group.

Yvonne Cranstoun has been involved with preschool play-groups for many years, and was a founder of the group in her own village. She became a member of the Oxford Preschool Research Group after taking part in the practitioner semi-nars held to help formulate research strategy, and was one of the first to try the recording techniques on which this book is based. She now combines tutoring a foundation course for the PPA with work, with Linnet McMahon, on the Rowntree project for making and disseminating teaching materials based on the Oxford findings.

The Oxford Preschool Research Project

1. *Under Five in Britain,* Jerome Bruner
2. *Childwatching at Playgroup and Nursery School,* Kathy Sylva, Carolyn Roy and Marjorie Painter
3. *Children and Minders,* Bridget Bryant, Miriam Harris and Dee Newton
4. *Children and Day Nurseries,* Caroline Garland and Stephanie White
5. *Working with Under Fives,* David Wood, Linnet McMahon and Yvonne Cranstoun
6. *Parents and Preschool,* Teresa Smith

Working with Under Fives

David Wood, Linnet McMahon
and Yvonne Cranstoun

THE
HIGH/SCOPE
PRESS

First published in England (1980) by
Grant McIntyre Ltd
39 Great Russell Street
London WC1B 3PH

**THE
HIGH/SCOPE
PRESS**
a division of
High/Scope Educational Research Foundation
600 North River Street
Ypsilanti, MI 48197
(313) 485-2000

Library of Congress Cataloging in
Publication Data

Wood, David J.
  Working with under fives.

  (Oxford preschool research project ; 5)
  Bibliography: p.
  Includes index.
  1. Nursery Schools. 2. Play groups.
I. McMahon, Linnet, joint author. II.
Cranstoun, Yvonne, joint author. III. Title.
IV. Series.

LB1140.2.W65   372'.216   80-27714

ISBN 0-931114-13-6

Contents

Foreword by Jack Wrigley   vii
Foreword by Jerome Bruner   ix
Acknowledgements   xi
Prologue   xiii

1 Adults and children   1
2 Three case studies: developing the method of research   12
3 Working in the preschool   34
4 Conversations with the preschool child   52
5 The language of the preschool   82
6 'Teaching' the young child   103
7 Adults at play   126
8 Can adults change?   162
9 The child-centred adult   190

Appendix A   Using transcripts and coding systems for group dissemination   211
Appendix B   Analysis of functions   228
Appendix C   Analysing conversations   233
Appendix D   Topics and domains of discourse   248

Short bibliography   253

Index   255

Foreword by Jack Wrigley

In 1971, when a massive expansion of nursery education in Britain was proposed, there was relatively little easily available evidence to suggest how best this should be done. Consequently the Department of Education and Science and the Scottish Education Department initiated a programme of research on nursery education to answer practical questions about provision and to study the effects of expansion. The Educational Research Board of the Social Science Research Council saw the need for a complementary research programme concerned as well with some more fundamental issues which covered the whole range of preschool education.

The work was coordinated in the Department of Education and Science by a management committee on which the Schools Council and SSRC were represented. The original idea, that SSRC should concentrate on fundamental research while DES funded more policy oriented and practical work, proved too simple. What quickly emerged was a view that much of the fundamental work on preschool children had already been carried out. What was lacking was the dissemination of that knowledge and its implementation in the field. Within SSRC a preschool working group was given the task of commissioning projects, and the work of the Oxford Preschool Research Group, under Professor Bruner, reported in this series of publications, was the main element in the first phase of the SSRC programme.

Professor Bruner had already accomplished distinguished fundamental work in this field and was therefore well placed to make the point of the need for dissemination and implementation. Despite the many changes in the economic and political scene in the 1970s, the original gap in knowledge remains important and the results of the SSRC research programme will do much to fill the gap. In particular, Professor Bruner's work in Oxfordshire has great value for the rest of the country. The publications of the Oxford Preschool Research Group, together with the results from other participants in the programme, will help give a firmer base on which to build for the future.

Jack Wrigley
Chairman
SSRC Educational Research Board Panel on
Accountability in Education
London, 1979

Foreword by Jerome Bruner

This book is one in a series that emerges from the Oxford Preschool Research Group. Like the others in the series, it is concerned with the provision of care in Britain for the preschool child away from home and is the result of several years of research devoted to various aspects of that issue. There are few more controversial and crucial issues facing Britain today. The objective of the series is to shed light on present needs, on the quality of care available and on the extent to which this care meets these needs. The general aim is to provide a basis for discussion of future policy.

The studies have all been financed by the Social Science Research Council of Great Britain. They were commissioned in 1974, just a year or two after Mrs Thatcher's White Paper, *Education: a Framework for Expansion*, was published, at a time when it was thought that there would be a publicly financed expansion of preschool care and education in Britain. Since that time events have caught up with the enterprise and Britain finds itself in a period of economic stringency during which many of the hoped-for changes will have to be shelved until better days come again. Nonetheless, the studies are opportune, for careful study and planning will be necessary not only to meet present needs with reduced resources, but to shape policy and practice for an improved future service on behalf of children in Britain and their families.

Developmental studies of the past two decades have pointed increasingly to the importance of the opening years of life for the intellectual, social, and emotional growth of human beings. The books in this series, it is hoped, shed light on the practical steps that must be taken to ensure that the early years can contribute to the well-being of a next generation in Britain.

Jerome Bruner

Oxford, 1979.

Acknowledgements

We are indebted to the 24 playgroup workers and nursery teachers, their children and colleagues for taking part in this demanding research. Needless to say, without their enthusiasm, dedication and insight this work could never have taken place. We are also indebted to Dr Heather Wood, who only escaped joint authorship for the many hours of work she put into the development of coding systems and statistical analysis because of her own reluctance to share any credit for the research. David Wood is also indebted to the Nuffield Foundation who, with the Social Science Research Council, enabled him to work full-time for a year in Oxford on the project. We also acknowledge our debt to Miss Penny Radcliffe for her efforts and patience in typing the manuscript.

Prologue

This book presents an analysis of approximately one thousand five hundred minutes of talk and interaction between nursery teachers and playgroup leaders with the children in their care. The analyses are based on recordings made – and often edited – by the practitioners themselves. Each practitioner made half-hour recordings in her own classroom or playgroup. These were designed to capture 'typical' segments of her day. They were busy half-hours, as we shall see. They were also very different half-hours – underlying each adult's activities were quite different types of interactions with children. Our main aim in this book is to explore and describe these differences and to try to work out some of the effects they have on the preschoolers involved.

The majority of practitioners, having discussed analyses of their documentary recordings, went on to make more experimental tapes, in which they tried to modify or develop their styles to reveal different facets of their work or to try out new ideas as to how they might encourage more sustained (and perhaps interesting and valuable) interactions with children. These helped us to etch out some of the problems facing the adult who tries to work profitably with the young. Not all the experiments worked, though some did. The 'failures', however, were as informative as the successes. They helped us to see, for example, how easy it is to move beyond the child's reach and understanding, stultifying him with adult demands that he is neither interested in nor capable of understanding. They also help us to uncover some aspects of 'good' conversational styles with young children.

Before we move into the background of the study, however, and then on to the way in which researchers and practitioners worked together and what they discovered, the following narrative account will, we hope, give some feel for the types of activities we will be looking at. This account is in no way typical of the recordings, for these varied widely from adult to adult. We have selected it because it illustrates the tremendous amount and variety of work that adults are involved in, and the great demands that are put on their energy and intelligence. All that follows took place in just over 25 minutes – and the teacher involved judged them to be a pretty typical slice of her day, working with under-fives.

Twenty-five minutes in the life of a nursery teacher

An afternoon session at the nursery school is just starting. The teacher, Rebecca, is in the classroom after two days away from the school. The children come in and are 'settling down to do some work'. Rebecca sees one child, Daniel, standing by the paints and goes over to him. But Sally is already occupying the painting platform, though she is just finishing a painting. Rebecca asks if that is her second one (she's allowed to do two) and is drawn into a conversation. Sally has folded the painting to give a symmetrical pattern – a butterfly. After admiring the painting, Rebecca asks Sally if Daniel may now have a turn. She tells Daniel to get an apron meanwhile. Then she starts to hang up the children's paintings.

A child comes over complaining that his toy train has come apart. Rebecca helps out and then uses the train and contents to form a play theme. This involves some consideration as to why one of the figures which goes with the train can stand up but not lie down – because of its size. They talk about why the man should want to lie down rather than stand up. Simon comes over; Rebecca greets him and admires his jumper. She then returns to Sally to find that the painting was, in fact, her first and that she has the option on another. Daniel is temporarily out of earshot, but has his apron on. Another child asks to paint and Rebecca promises he can when the others have finished.

Then, she sees one of the bigger boys on one of the smaller toy horses and asks him to stop, explaining that he's too big for it. Daniel has drifted away from the painting corner to play with bricks. One of the children waiting to paint points out that he's wearing an apron and not painting. Rebecca explains that one must wear it to paint but can wear it to do other things if one wishes. She helps Sally get down from the painting platform and catches sight of Sarah's creation, which they briefly discuss. Sally has dirty hands and Rebecca suggests she go and wash them. Meanwhile Daniel has taken up the painting and she goes to help him sign it (speedy painter, that Daniel). She asks him where he wants his name, top or bottom. Daniel decides it would look good along the side! They start to discuss Daniel's painting – a car with no wheels. Esther comes up and asks Rebecca to be her granny in the home corner. Rebecca promises to do so when they've finished the analysis of Daniel's car with no wheels. Then comes signature time and a discussion of how paint tends to get on arms if one signs at the top of wet paintings. Daniel opts to do another painting. Meanwhile, Sally is struggling to hang hers up. They decide to turn Daniel's painting upside down as a solution to the problem of signing at the top without getting one's arm wet in the paint. Meanwhile Sally tries to appropriate one of Darrel's pictures. Rebecca suggests she uses another sheet for hers. Daniel is signed, sealed and hung up.

Esther, looking for the promised granny, asks Rebecca to knock on the door of the Wendy house. Rebecca asks her to wait and redresses the children who have finished painting. She looks to the two boys who had the trains and asks where the trains are and if they've been put away. She gets three children together to make 'tack patterns', pushing coloured tacks into a foam base. Then she goes to fulfil her promise to Esther.

Knocking on the door of the Wendy house, she announces that granny has arrived. Esther pours out her theme. She's made dinner for granny, is absolutely swamped with hungry babies, and she did manage in spite of all the pressures to prepare a meal. Rebecca enters into her role and they discuss the problems of feeding babies and getting them to sleep. Do babies eat dinner? As they talk, other children start to arrive, including a relative newcomer who hovers on the threshold. Rebecca draws them into a tea-party, suggesting that one be dad and he lay the table (a push towards emancipation?). This becomes quite elaborate. Gavin arrives made up with moustache, Oxford United jumper and toy watch. Interposed with the dinner party Rebecca takes time to discuss time and how watches go round, to point at numbers and so on. They discuss how to make her watch and the toy one look the same to tell the same time. Two girls come in and bring their tack patterns to show her. They talk about how they look alike if put side by side. Then starts a discussion of differences in colour between the two creations and Rebecca gets them each to count how many rows they have. The children become enthusiastic and start to talk about why they hadn't both used the same coloured tacks – the black ran out.

Daniel brings his second painting which got splashed, Rebecca asks Esther to excuse her and she goes to sign Daniel's painting, promising to come back for more dinner later on. They discuss Daniel's painting; he too has folded his – to produce a 'spider'. Then follows another chat about how we can produce a symmetrical pattern by folding the paper in half so that the painted part meets with the clean part. It's signed along the side and, another masterpiece duly authored, Rebecca makes her way back to the Wendy house as promised to finish dinner.

Rebecca is back in the Wendy house with five children. Daniel, having finished his painting, returns with her to join the others. The table is being laid and people are being presented with plates, saucers and the like, with impressive courtesy . . . 'Mrs King', says the irrepressible Esther, 'I'm Mummy,' Rebecca suggests that Mummy and baby should take a rest! One of the children comments on how easily the plastic plates break and Rebecca agrees that they aren't very strong. Gavin arrives and needs a plate. Several are enjoined to search one out for him. 'Mrs King,' Esther again with news about the baby. Rebecca suggests she has a bottle. They start to serve out sausages, bacon and so on and Rebecca helps ensure that all get a portion. Another child approaches her with a painting. A cage with lions. There follows a discussion of the problems in housing lions. 'Mummy, would you hold the baby?' Esther again. Rebecca agrees and addresses Jamie about his dinner. Then it's time for her to go, so she bids farewell, promising to visit them again sometime.

She goes back to the painting corner where Ian is painting a figure. They talk about the need for legs to end in feet. Beatrice arrives looking for sustenance and Rebecca tells her where to get her milk. Another child is painting apples and Sarah is finishing yet another painting. Rebecca suggests she put it in her folder. Then she goes up to Owen and tells him she wants to do something with him. He's a bit sandy so she gives him the brush off. Katy would like to come too and so Rebecca takes both along to a table where she gets them to sit down. Yes, of course Daniel can come too, though there is a bit of a problem arranging the seating. 'Mrs King,' Esther again with the baby. She decides to go 'home'.

Rebecca turns back to Katy, Owen and Daniel and they start to talk once again about symmetry. 'Could you make some symmetrical patterns like these on your peg board?' she asks. Owen is still black and sandy. She asks them to pass different coloured tacks to her and she tells them her plan for the design. Now let's see if Katy can make one like that. But she needs help and gets it. A call from the loo, Suzanne hasn't quite got the bottom-wiping skill mastered and Rebecca goes over. They discuss her clothes, then she is dressed and they go to wash their hands. Then Suzanne is taken off for her milk, Rebecca returns to the discussion about symmetry – the subject of an earlier lesson. The tape ends as they decide whether to put the name on another painting along the top or the bottom!

What different roles is Rebecca fulfilling in these various encounters with children? How are we to describe her work with the under-fives? How do her roles and styles differ from those fulfilled by others working in similar situations? More important, what are the children actually gaining from her work with them? What benefit do they derive from her involvement in their play, her attempts to tell them something about time, number and symmetry? These are the family of questions we explore in the following pages.

1
Adults and children

This book – number five in a series which reports on pre-school care in Oxfordshire – appears, like its sister volumes, at a time of mounting debate about the State's part in and support for under-fives and their families. The same Government, indeed some of the same politicians, that introduced *Education: a Framework for Expansion* for nursery care in 1972, now seem determined to preside over the atrophy, if not destruction, of State provision. The primary cause, of course, is an economic one. But it is interesting that the theory of child care changes so systematically with the gross national product, while the nature of children, one suspects, remains the same. When women are needed in the work-force, their children become the responsibility of all, and the virtues of equal opportunity, the benefits of professional care and the advantage of good facilities for the disadvantaged, are underlined. As the workforce shrinks and women be-come somewhat of an embarrassment in commerce and industry, the immense value of 'maternal' support comes to the fore; and that children should stay where they belong – in a childminder's home if not their own – becomes crucial to early development. As the State with-draws, the vitality and flexibility of local, cheap care is underlined by politicians, and the advantages of care in the community become tremendously valuable.

Oxfordshire, where this work began, was among the first to halt its expansion of nursery care and then cut its provision. Meanwhile throughout the country, letters to editors, meetings of teachers' unions, marches of mothers, act like social thermometers, marking the rise in the temper-ature of debate. In the *Nottingham Evening Post*, following on the loss of nursery assistants in Nottinghamshire schools, learned individuals wrote scorning the teacher who was so incompetent professionally that she could not, single-handed, care for a paltry 30 or so children.

There are theories to help too. We might rather mis-guidedly call on Piaget and others who emphasize the importance of the child's commerce with nature, materials and his peers to support the case for fewer adults in preschool care. Where one holds the view that children develop naturally through a succession of universal stages, and are best left to their own devices and the company of their age mates, it seems to follow quite logically that a single adult, hiding in the shadows of the classroom and simply providing the materials of development, should suffice. Other pundits advocate turning the clock back, placing at the feet of 'progressive education' responsibility for declining standards, unruly behaviour and other social and educational ills. If we abandon the silly, romantic notion that the child best decides what he should be doing, when and with whom, we can get the whole class back in their seats, working at their desks. How much easier the task of managing a group when they are all quietly working away at the same tasks. Think how many teachers and would-be teachers we can put back into really productive work if we rid ourselves of the silly notion that children should not be regimented and drilled. One teacher could quite easily manage a group of malleable, easily-controlled, geriatric babies, if only we got them all back to their desks and onto a good, central curriculum. And standards would rise too. We could get them all reading, writing and thinking that much earlier if we only stuck to the job of telling them all what to do and ensuring that they get on with it. The 'whole child' would not suffer if we concentrated on teaching him skills. We can always find theories of the child to support action arising out of the economic condition of the State.

This is not a polemical book. It starts out with no grand theory of child development, no great design for education and no Utopian methods for bringing the young child to maturity – by cheap or expensive routes. But it will reflect back on political questions about the proper level of provision for the young.

In essence, it is a book about 24 practitioners – nursery teachers and playgroup workers – and the children in their charge. Early care of the young in groups under the management of relative strangers is still a new experiment. Children are developing and learning in situations that previous generations – including that of their own parents – have not experienced. Women, many of them without any formal training, are working with under-fives in a way none has worked before. What demands do they meet, what do the preschoolers need for healthy, happy growth in groups and how do adults respond? How natural and effective is care for the young child in these essentially public situations? Is it simply an extension of mothering, or does the new experiment in child care breed unique problems and demand the development of a new, human technology for meeting them? This is the sort of question we address in the following pages.

But how are we to proceed? What should we be looking for, how should we describe what we see in nursery schools and playgroups? And who should do the looking? How do we go about the task of developing a language, a set of terms which pull out the common tasks of group care and the differences in style of working between different practitioners? Above all, how are we to try to evaluate what we find and what should we seek to change?

We are by no means the first to tackle such questions, though our knowledge of the preschool situation and the way adults and children behave in them is still sparse. The pioneering work of Joan Tough and of the Tizards and their colleagues at the Thomas Coram Research Unit in London has opened our eyes to many features of preschool care and its effects on the young, and there is a growing volume of research in the United States, much of it addressed, like our own Educational Priority Area studies, to the issue of disadvantaged children and how they can be given a Head Start in life. We shall draw on some the findings from these studies in this chapter – not to provide a comprehensive overview, however, merely to show how existing knowledge helped to shape the way in which we worked in our own research.

First, however, we need to say a little about the origins of this particular element of the Oxford Preschool Research Project and its relationships to its sister studies. Although the findings of our work with practitioners stand on their own and will not be cross-referenced in any detail to the other work, the direction that we took and the methods we developed were designed to complement the other studies. Our nearest relative is *Childwatching in Playgroup and Nursery School* by Kathy Sylva, Carolyn Roy and Marjorie Painter (1980). This is an extremely detailed and extensive study of children at work and play in preschools both in Oxfordshire and in Miami, Florida. It involved detailed observations and descriptions of the activities of some 120 children in Oxfordshire, observed individually over twenty-minute periods as they went about life in their preschool groups. Sylva and her colleagues examined the child's play, his contacts with peers and adults, the relationships between different types of material and the extent and complexity of his activities, his experiences in organized, adult-led activities and many other facets of his time in groups.

In this volume, we focus more squarely on the adult and her experiences. However, our main aim in doing so is to try to discover the effects of different styles of working with children on the experiences of the children and the part that they, in turn, play in interactions with the practitioners. Are there any general principles to be discovered which will help people who work with the under-fives achieve their own objectives more effectively?

If we are to describe what adults set about and how effective they believe themselves to be in achieving their objectives with young children, we need some insights into their goals and aspirations. What do they think the pre-schooler should gain from his experience with them?

How do we gain access to practitioners' aspirations and ideals? Well, we can, of course, ask them. And this has already been done, though not in Oxfordshire where we undertook our study. In one investigation 500 teachers were canvassed in an attempt to establish what their major aims were in looking after children (Taylor, Exon and Holley, 1972). The list was as follows:

1 Socio-emotional development
2 Intellectual development
3 Creation of an effective transition from home to school
4 Aesthetic development
5 Physical development

There is a striking measure of similarity between this list and the next, which is based on the replies of playgroup leaders in another study (Turner, 1977):

1 Socio-emotional development
2 Intellectual development
3 Settling into school
4 Physical development
5 Aesthetic development

And when we look at what parents hope their children will gain from being in those same playgroups we find another close fit:

1 Socio-emotional development
2 Help in starting school
3 Cognitive development
4 Physical development
5 Aesthetic development

But what is the relationship between such attitudes, expressed with relative calm and detachment in answering a questionnaire, and actual behaviour in the heat and noise of the preschool? More generally, what is the relationship between our ideals and our actions? The connection is far from easy to establish. In Turner's study, for example, when the playgroup leaders were actually observed, to discover how they spent their time, it turned out that they spent eight times more of their time in the development of cognitive skills than they did on socio-emotional development.

But are we right to equate time with priority? And perhaps interactions with a child during learning and teaching also have an element of socio-emotional development. Perhaps encounters dedicated to helping a child establish and maintain happy relationships with others are fleeting – resting on a smile or a wink easily overlooked by an outsider but of tremendous significance to the child for whom it is intended. At another level, it is surely the case that much of our behaviour is not premeditated or consciously guided by long term aspirations. It is often a reaction to circumstances, thought about, if at all, as it is done. Most of our commonplace behaviour goes on without much forethought or planning; only the unusual, surprising and problematic plunges us into thought. And our encounters with children are of a commonplace, everyday nature. So asking is not enough. It may inform us about aspirations but tell us little about what people actually do in trying to fulfil them. And since our emphasis here is on the extent to which methods match goals – how far a teacher's or playgroup worker's activities actually work in getting her where she wants to be – we clearly needed to go beyond the interview situation.

Another central consideration in the relationships between goals and actions is the fact that practitioners have *many* goals. None of the short list mentioned above was ruled out as unimportant – so the preschool adult has a real problem of managing herself and her situation so that all of them can be met. And they may well come into conflict. To teach a young child effectively, to find out what and how he thinks about something, or to try and take him further in his understanding of other people, may well conflict with the socio-emotional needs of others in the group of children. In his choice of play a child may well, through noise or physical intrusion, disrupt the more sedate activities of others. In short, while we may have many things we want to achieve, we can only do one thing at a time.

So we must plan and manage. Either we must rely on

others to take care of remaining goals or we must organize our behaviour over time to make sure that we do justice to them all. As we shall see, this meeting of goals through the management of resources became one of our central interests.

Do adults matter?

None of the practitioners who worked with us seriously doubted the importance of their impact on the children. Indeed, one of their major reasons for getting involved in the research was to find out more about themselves, their styles and their effects on children. In our discussions and analyses, theirs was the voice of experience. Few of the psychologists on the team had had any real experience of children in groups; their contribution to discussion and debate was a knowledge of the literature about the abilities of this age group plus a knowledge of previous and of ongoing work elsewhere which was starting to produce general hypotheses about the nature and effects of preschool life on the developing child. The meeting of these two sorts of knowledge about children gave birth to the various systems for describing and evaluating adult–child relationships which we offer in the following chapters. What are these general hypotheses about the impact of preschool experience and how did they help shape the way in which we worked together?

During the 1960s some psychologists, sociologists, linguists and educators became preoccupied – some would say obsessed – by the relationships between children's social backgrounds, their language and their school performance. It was a well-documented fact that children from working-class backgrounds tended to do less well in school than those from the middle classes, and it was suggested that the roots of these differences in attainment rested upon the different language experiences of children in the early years of life. Basically, it was argued that some children were well prepared for school life and school language, and others not.

Thus, the basis of poor achievement and all the related problems of education was supposed to be found in the linguistic disadvantages of working-class culture.

From these theories about the social origins of disadvantage arose a range of intervention programmes. Head Start in the United States and our own Educational Priority Areas, were designed, in part, to compensate for the supposed deficiencies of working-class life.

Such projects met with mixed success. The first studies suggested that while it was possible to raise the achievements of children through intensive preschool intervention, any effects found tended to disappear once the child went into normal schools. However, other, more carefully constructed evaluations have since revealed lasting effects. But a major ingredient of success seems to lie in continuous support, or in changing not only the attitudes and abilities of the child but also those of his family or local culture. In other words, if the social framework within which the child is reared is not changed in line with the new experiences he receives in preschool care, where his later school experience does not build upon his preschool life (Weikart, 1978), the impact will not last.

The major implication of this work – mirrored recently in studies of much older children in secondary schools (Rutter *et al.*, 1979) – is that differences between children at school and in other public situations are modifiable to a certain extent by exposing the child and perhaps his family to new experiences. The suggestion that lasting success hinges on the creation of changes in the social framework of the child's life also adds some significance to the efforts of many people in preschool care to involve parents too in preschool life (see Smith, 1980).

Other recent research, however, has seriously challenged the notion that the seeds of disadvantage at school lie in an impoverished linguistic background in the home. Barbara Tizard and her colleagues (1980), for example, have examined the language and interactions experienced by working- and middle-class children at home and at nursery school.

They found very marked differences in the children's experiences at school. The working-class children were less likely to be found in extended interactions with their teachers; the language they heard tended to take the form of questions from teacher. They asked fewer questions themselves and tended to approach adults more for purposes of management than to solicit contact, conversation or involvement. Middle-class children were not managed so much and were questioned less frequently; and they themselves asked more questions.

Many of these differences, however, were not so evident at home. Working-class children at home were just about as likely to be involved in extended interactions with mothers, be asked questions and so forth, as were their middle-class age mates. This suggests, then, that the differences we observe between children at school are not strongly mirrored in their home experiences. Other studies, which have examined the language of home, have yielded similar conclusions (e.g. Wells, 1978).

It seems unlikely, then, that the different impacts of preschool care on children from different sections of society rest in any easily identified linguistic deficit transmitted by parents and brought into the school. There is something to do with the young working-class child's reaction to the preschool situation itself that produces the dramatic deficit in his apparent competence, compared to his performances at home. Whatever the reasons for these differences, and we discuss some candidates later in the book, it seems to be the case that the nature of the relationships between practitioners and their children differs in a way that reflects, among other things, the children's home backgrounds. But do these differences really matter? Does the greater frequency of teacher questions to some children than to others, or the greater incidence of management experienced by some preschoolers, make any difference to their development? Evidence from our study and others suggests that they do indeed matter a great deal. In a study mounted in Northern Ireland, Turner found that some children in the preschool tended to be managed more than others. Adults with such children were more concerned with the initiation or control of their behaviour than they were, say, in chatting with them, playing with them, or instructing them. Taylor also found a strong relationship between the type of contact that the child received from the adults and his level of language ability measured in tests. In short, children who were managed more appeared the least competent in measures of language ability. Taylor suggests a causal link between the two; children who receive more interactions with practitioners proceed better in their language development.

Other studies have also underlined the importance of the nature and quality of adult–child interactions in the pre-school. In one, Karnes and his colleagues (1972) looked at the effects of four different preschool philosophies on the development of groups of children of similar backgrounds. One was a Montessori based programme, another a community group dedicated to the goal of integrating children from different social backgrounds. A third was a 'traditional' nursery school, and the fourth an experimental group set up on the basis of principles derived from psychological studies of child development. Karnes found that the four programmes exerted marked and different effects on children's achievements. Children in the experimental programme fare best on measures of their language ability and intelligence, for example, showing a significant increase in ability over children in other programmes. The researchers concluded that what seemed to mark the most successful programmes from the less successful ones was the nature of the relationships established between adult and child. Where a programme encouraged adult and child to work together, on occasion, in a one-to-one fashion; where the adult concerned herself with individual children's activities and language and was involved with them in doing things jointly, then those children tended to fare well. Where children were left more to their own devices and expected to learn continually from their own unaided efforts, they fared less well.

There are now a number of different items of evidence that

point in a common direction. Sustained interactions between adult and child, in which the adult acts in the service of the child's ideas and actions, exert a positive effect on a variety of measures of the child's developing competence.

But there is a danger in accepting such findings uncritically. In the first place, research to date has only tried to evaluate a rather narrow range of cognitive and linguistic functions. The child's social development, personal happiness and aesthetic appreciation have been less intensively studied, though there is no reason to suppose that these should necessarily be subject to different factors. A more important danger, underlined by the work of Sylva and her colleagues, lies in the limited adult resources in the preschool. It would not be practical (and probably not advisable) to suggest that each child should be given long periods of sustained attention by an adult. Where an adult is faced with a largish group of children, and is motivated, perhaps, to increase her personal involvement with them, she may push herself into more directed group activities. Sylva's research suggests that such organized activities may well produce uninterested, passive children. Our own research, as we shall see, points in a similar direction. Our practitioners (like indeed, the literature on preschool care itself), do show consciousness of the potential pitfalls of too much adult control over the young child's activity. In fact, they often effectively preclude themselves from protracted involvement with the children at all.

The practical question we must ask, given that practitioners accept the importance of their interactions with the child, is whether they are able to translate their desires for interaction into effective practice. If their ability to achieve their objectives with children largely depends on the nature of their contacts with them, *can* they in fact set up interactions with children that are not too controlling and stultifying? If so, which abilities and characteristics make this possible?

2
Three case studies: developing the method of research

Adults in both the playgroup movement and in nursery education demand a lot of themselves. Their aspirations for what their children are to gain from preschool experience are numerous and pitched high, as we saw in Chapter 1. But the real issue is how these aspirations come to fruition – how are good intentions translated into effective practice? What goals compatible with those listed in Chapter 1 are being fulfilled in the following excerpt for example?

At the painting table
    c: I've finished my painting now.
    a: Oh, that's nice. Go and put it near your peg – go on, good boy. Jilly, I hope you're going to put that apron on if you want to paint. Not so much noise, please, Nigel. A bit quieter please. Yes, you can paint quietly.
    c: This is the biggest car what I made.
    a: Oh, the biggest car. Go and wash your hands dear.
    c: I'm not going to wash mine.
    a: OK, don't wash yours then.
    Janet, have you had your milk dear? No, well go and get it then, before it's all gone.
    John I think you'd better go and get a tissue for that nose of yours. There's one in the loo. Off you go.

Here, the primary function of the adults' interactions with children is clearly managerial. Of itself, management furthers no educational goals for the child, although effective control and distribution of opportunities is obviously a vital part of any successful preschool care. Good husbandry of resources is what makes possible all the other, more social and educational activities. But what is good management? What is the right level of adult control over children's experiences? When does the pursuit of harmony and smooth-running spill over into unnecessary interference and arbitrary direction?

Even where the objectives behind the teacher or play-group worker's actions are clear and intuitively compatible with one or more of the general goals itemized in the last chapter, the styles and methods that different practitioners exhibit in trying to fulfil them vary enormously, as in the following.

Hot bananas

c:	And I like bananas.
a:	Bananas – Oh, where do you get those from?
c1:	I don't know.
a:	You don't know? Do *you* know where you get bananas from?
c:	The shop.
a:	The shop (pause) yes (pause) and they grow . . . in a hot country don't they? (no response)
c:	He's a coal lorry!
a:	He's the coal lorry; what does the coal lorry do then?
c and c1:	Brings coal.
c:	They put sacks, put sacks . . .
a:	In sacks?
c:	That's sacks to put it in.
a:	And what's in the sacks?
c:	Coal.
a:	Does your mummy have coal? . . . Does she? (no response). Have you got a coal fire? To keep you warm?
c:	Hmm . . . they put it down. (I think he's playing here)
c1:	We got a fire in our house.

A: You've got a coal fire have you? Does
        mummy have to light it? What does she light
        it with?

c1:   Turns it on (very quietly)

A: She turns it on, does she? Oh well – you don't
        put paper and sticks on and then coal . . . to
        light it . . . no.

c and c1: No, we have to do it this way.

c: Next . . . next time I'm going to have another
        birthday.

Bristol Zoo

c: There's a zoo in Bristol, isn't there?

A: There is a zoo, yes.

c: Have you been to it?

A: Once, a long time ago when I was a little girl I went
   to it.

c: Oh.

A: Do you go to it sometimes when you go to your
   Grannie's?

c: Yes, we might go . . . daddy said we can go to the
   seaside or the . . . uhh – or the zoo – uhh, when we
   go there.

A: Oh, that would be lovely. Which do you think you'd
   rather go to?

c: Ahmmm . . . the zoo?

A: The zoo. It's nicer than the seaside, isn't it?

c: Hmm, I think it's nicer. No I'd like to go to the
   seaside first and bring some shells – to granny and
   pampam, still I brought some for them last time –
   might bring some more.

A: S'pect they were very pleased.

c: Hm, they were.

A: I like to find shells. There are lots of different sorts of
   shells at the seaside, aren't there?

c: Yes.

A: Different shapes, and . . .

c: (interrupts) might be a crab, or . . . or a hmm
. . . starfish.

a: Might.

c: But these sting don't they?

a: Umm. Starfish?

c: Yes, starfish, might.

a: Yes, I think they can if you poke them – it's best to leave them alone isn't it?

c: Hmm. Once I had one in a bucket and I was so scared (it was crawling up) – so very carefully, as I was about, I threw it in the sea.

Do such differences in style matter? Is one more likely to help children further along in their development of social awareness, linguistic skills or aesthetic appreciation than the other? Perhaps such differences in approach are irrelevant. And what about the children involved? Are the various styles exhibited by the adults in these recordings due to the fact, say, that some of the children are more mature than others? Or maybe it is the case that the children come from quite different social backgrounds? Who is in charge of the child – nature or the adult?

This list of questions and some answers to them, as we said in Chapter 1, form the major focus of this book. We examine the various roles that adults fill in their attempts to bring their ideals to life, and the different styles and methods they exhibit in doing so. Then we try to unravel some of the effects these differences exert over the experiences and development of children.

While this set of questions and objectives were always in the background of our research, the methods we used in trying to achieve them were not. These were created in an extended, frank and sometimes argumentative relationship between three practitioners (two nursery teachers and a playgroup supervisor) and a psychologist. This working relationship and the methods of research and analysis to which it gave rise are the principal foci of this chapter.

From observation to participation

During the first year of the work of the Oxford Preschool Research Group, members of the group had started detailed and extensive observations of children in playgroups and nursery schools (now come to fruition and written up by Sylva, Roy and Painter, 1980). At the end of that year, we were given the opportunity to organize a series of in-service training days to which nursery teachers and playgroup workers were invited. Some seventy or so turned up to each meeting in the depths of an extremely inhospitable winter. We took the opportunity to present to them our data on the behaviour of preschoolers, some of whom were in their classes. The meetings did not go very well. This was mainly due to our style of presentation – which was rather formal and numerical. But for one teacher at least – we will call her Janet – there were deeper reasons for her feeling that we had missed something in our work to that point. While information about children's patterns of behaviour in preschools could hardly be more relevant to anyone considering their effectiveness as a teacher or playgroup worker, the observations left one vital perspective unexplored – the perceptions and intentions of the adults actually working with the children. Janet had already allowed observers into her class to see her children at work and play. She spoke to the psychologist on the team along the following lines.

> All the time the observer was coding* the children's behaviour I kept wanting to get hold of her and say 'Look, this is happening for a reason, things are not this way by accident but because we feel that certain things should happen'.

I think she was resenting the submersion of 'her' children's activities into a general picture – one which lost the deeper

* The 'coding' referred to is a list of categories representing the major activities in which children get involved in preschools. The list was developed by Sylva and her colleagues in consultation with practitioners (Sylva *et al.*, 1980). Observers watched individual children in nursery schools and playgroups and coded their behaviour into these categories.

structure of her efforts, her intentions and reasons. The aim of these observations, of course, was to achieve a general picture of children's activities; they were not addressed to the question of the relationships between teacher philosophy and children's activities.

Our interest in looking at adults, however, mirrored Janet's. We wanted to see what impact different styles of working with the under-fives had on the experiences and activities of the children. We also wanted to discover whether the relationships between such styles and their effects were compatible with the adults' own view of themselves and their objectives. Would playgroup workers and teachers discover anything of value about themselves and their techniques, which might help them to work differently and, in their own eyes, more effectively in the future?

But how were we to translate this aspiration into a method of research? Interviews and questionnaires would not get at the relationships between philosophy and behaviour. We also ruled out the possibility of actually observing the practitioners as they went about their tasks, feeling this might be too disruptive. We could not be continually stopping them in mid-flight to ask what they were doing and why. Eventually, we hit on another idea. We would provide teachers and playgroup workers with portable tape-recorders and small, powerful microphones. They could then record whatever they wished of their work, adding any commentary they might want to make about why they had done what they did and what they felt about the outcome.

Taking this step clearly meant that we had relinquished a good deal of control over the data. Each practitioner would approach the recording task in her own way. Some, as we will find, simply switched the tape on and left it recording until it ran out. Others selected their material piecemeal. Some gave extensive commentaries, others none at all. These variations meant that we would have to be extremely cautious in interpreting the general nature of what we found. In particular, while we might legitimately look at relationships between what adults and children said on the recordings, we could not assume that the tapes were necessarily representative of more general adult–child relationships, though we did develop ways of trying to find out just how far the practitioners could vary their style, as we shall see in Chapter 8.

In the early days of the project, two teachers – Janet and another – we will call her Rebecca – made their first recordings. We transcribed these and took the first steps towards trying to analyse them. Initially, we simply read through the transcripts trying to specify what the adult was attempting to do – the functions she was trying to fulfil. Eventually, we came up with some 26 different categories of adult behaviour which enabled us to code every utterance on the transcript. Both teachers were sent copies of the transcripts together with the initial analyses, and we met several times thereafter to discuss them. We eventually came up with the information shown in Figure 2.1. These were devised to show each teacher how she had divided her time between the various functions we had identified. As you will see, the two teachers share some common features but in other ways are quite different.

Janet		Rebecca	
Function	Percentage	Function	Percentage
Directs	30	Elaborates play	15
Gives information	9	Describes things	13
Monitors	8	Directs	11
Asks about intention	6	Gives Instruction	10
Evaluates	6	Monitors	9
Agrees	5	Asks for information	6
Indicates own intention	5	Asks for description	5
Asks for information	4	Gives information	5
Repeats	4	Asks about intention	4
Gives instruction	4	Negotiates	4

Figure 2.1 *Percentages of Janet's and Rebecca's time spent in different activities*

Janet's tape was quite high in management activities, as illustrated in the following excerpt from the recordings.

Following through

A: Do you want me to do some writing on this for you?

C: My name.

A: Your name, alright?

C: . . . cat.

A: You want me to write a cat, hmm? Right. Where would you like me to do the writing? Right. A cat.

c1: I fell over.

A: You bumped yourself, Matthew?

c1: Yes . . . my knee.

A: Well, let me have a look at your knee. Lisa, I'll just put that there for a minute while I look at Matthew's knees. I haven't quite finished. Let me have a look at your knees. There's one knee. Where's the other knee? They feel alright.

c1: They not, not my hands, my hands not.

A: No?

c1: Going to play water.

A: Yes, that sounds a good idea. Get an apron then and I'll tie it up for you.

C: (inaudible)

A: Bring me an apron and I'll tie it up. One of the blue ones, yes. Now Lisa, L–I–S–A. Lisa. A cat Lisa. You can put it on the third shelf down there, where the other pictures are.

c2: Can I do a painting?

A: There's a space there now, Ian.

c1: . . . the water.

A: Oh, you've changed your mind. Now, before you play in the water . . .

c1: What?

A: Run to the toilet?

c1: Yes.

A: And do a wee.

C: Yes

A: Alright? Shall I come with you!

C: Yes.

A: Yes, alright.

This was typical of much of Janet's tape. A good deal of her involvement with children was to do with providing services and management – directing children into the next activity; asking what they wanted to do next; tying aprons, soothing knees, negotiating and stopping potentially dangerous or threatening activities. Rebecca's tape was quite different in nature. Although she was occasionally occupied in management and services, a good deal of her time was spent in play and instruction – taking part in children's pretend activities in the Wendy corner, and in teaching them about number, symmetrical patterns and so forth.

The Wendy corner

A: Oh good, everybody got some? Oh, what about Jamie? Jamie hasn't got anything yet.

C: Oh, you could find it yourself, we're so busy.

c2: Yes. (inaudible)

A: I think we need those forks to eat with, Jamie.

C: I'll stick them in the . . . first.

A: Then you can set them out. Oh, Gavin that's lovely. Oh, I'm looking at it upside down, you'll have to turn it this way. It says half past one, hmm, it's a bit slow, my watch says quarter to two. I think it's time for school.

C: I . . . (inaudible)

A: Make it move round?

C: That goes . . .

A: No, can you turn it and show me? . . . Yes. Can you make it the same as that? Guess we haven't got all the numbers . . .

C: (interrupts) Look what I've done.

A: Oh, those are lovely, aren't they? Shall I come and look. (aside: two girls came to show me their patterns)

C: (interrupts) We got . . .

A: They're the same . . . yes, well, if you put them side by side, that one's the same, which other one is the same?

c: Ehh, the brown (?) No, brown.

A: (interrupts) both the browns (?)

c: (in parallel) . . . (?)

A: Those are, Jamie, yes, the blue and the green and the dark green. Do you know how many rows (?) they've got?

c: Yes.

A: Is that one at the top of yours . . . (inaudible) How many rows have you got? Can you count them?

c: 1 – 2 – 3 – 4 – 5 – 6 – 7 – 8 – 9 – 10.

A: How many rows have you got?

c: . . . 1 – 2 – 3 – 4 – 5 – 6 – 7 . . .

c2: (inaudible)

c: 8 – 9 – 10 – 11.

A: Hm, I think you counted one of them twice. So try again. (together) 1 – 2 – 3 – 4 – 5 – 6 – 7 – 8 – 9 – 10. Now there's something that's not quite the same about these two. See if you've seen what it is.

c: The white.

A: Well, apart from the colours being in different places. There's something else that's different.

c: That one . . .

A: Yes. (relieved?) Did you see that. (wider audience?)

c: I did that because I couldn't see any more black.

A: Oh, I see, so you finished it off with brown.

c: I did that with brown as well, look. (warming)

A: Yes, well you've got more browns than Norah, haven't you, but not so many blacks. Yes, they're very nice indeed. What are you going to do now? Are you going to take them out and do another one?

c: Yes.

c2: (parallel – Daniel) Going to do my name . . . it splashed.

c: This time.

c2: (parallel) Going to do my name in the white (?) and it . . . and it . . . had a big splash on it.

A: A splash?

c: Yes.

a: Is that the name that we did together just now? (aside: that was Daniel). Esther, will you excuse me a minute? I have to go and write Daniel's name on his painting. Can I come back and finish my dinner a bit later on? Thank you, Jamie, I have to go now, but I'll come back and finish my dinner later.

c: Yes.

a: Alright? What have you got Darryl (amused). You've got it on both sides too. Oh . . . goodness.

c: A spider.

a: It is like a spider.

Janet was clearly moved by the transcripts. We had several meetings and Janet frequently said that in spite of our analysis of functions she felt we had not grasped the essential nature of what she had set out to do. Her sense of what she was about failed to come through on her recording and our analysis. She said that one of her primary aims was, on occasion, to get involved with children to help them explore their ideas, feelings and experiences in some depth. There was none of this on the tape and the predominantly managerial impression that came over was thus not consistent with her sense of what she did as a teacher. Unfortunately, Janet fell ill about this time and this, combined with a change in staffing on the project which was to come, somewhat inhibited further contact.

One thing that we did explore in some depth, however, was the way in which the two teachers actually worked in the school. Janet, in a detailed letter to us, wrote:

> When considering the management activity of any classroom, I feel one must first examine the teacher's 'givens' in a particular establishment.

The school in which she worked was open plan linked with a pastoral system. Each teacher in the school 'owned' particular children and would see them with their parents both when they came to school and when they left each afternoon.

Throughout the day, the teacher remained responsible for her children – particularly for mothering services like toileting, changing, and soothing bumps and bruises. But she also remained responsible for particular 'territory' and for events going on in 'her' room. By combining an open plan (as much free choice from children as possible) and the mothering aspect of the pastoral system, the school hoped, in Janet's words:

> . . . that this system will allow both parents and children to focus on one particular staff member to give security within the open plan.

There were a number of timetabled activities – storytimes in morning and afternoon; music sessions and so forth. Many of these were optional, so that children did not have to go to them if they were involved with preferred activities of their own. But Janet still had the responsibility for letting her children know, say, that storytime was imminent, in order that they could exercise their right to choose. Consequently, she was quite often on the hoof around her pastoral domain, letting her children know what the time was – requesting intentions and giving directions as to where activities were located, as in the following:

Storytime
A: Are you going to story today, Matthew?
c: Yes.
c1: Is it your story?
A: It's my big story, but you'll be going to little story. Do you want to take off the water apron, then? Are you going to story?
cs: (in parallel – inaudible)
A: I don't know whose turn it is for little story, Matthew. I think it's Mrs Russell's turn. Well, shall I take off your apron?
c: Yes.
A: Yes.
c: Yes, if it's Mrs Wilson's turn.

A: Yes, if it's Mrs Wilson's turn. There you go now. (to all around in the garden) Storytime. Storytime, Haley. Storytime, James.

C: I'm doing something.

A: Yes, well could you finish what you're doing please if you want to come to story. Jonathan please don't throw that. It's only balls we throw.

C: Shall I come to story?

A: Yes, that sounds a good idea.

C: . . . bionic woman.

A: Storytime. Could you take the truck back off this muddy hill, please.

C: We're allowed on 'ere.

A: Are you allowed on there now?

C: Yes.

A: If it's stopped being too muddy. Storytime. It's storytime.

CS: (in turn) We're not coming.

A: Storytime, Philip.

C: Naaaa

T: Right.

She was often, then, spokesperson for the timetable. Management demands on her were increased by the fact that her children were highly mobile within a relatively large area – a number of rooms, gardens, etc. Consequently, if she had promised a child to do something for him, she often had quite a task of 'following through', searching him out, say, to tell him that the water table was now a little less crowded and had space for him . . .

(over the tape to DW) How to follow through with a boy you can't keep track of . . . (to her helper) Are you free for a minute Mrs Russell? Yes, well I'd like to go and find Matthew . . . I've misplaced Matthew . . . Matthew! . . . Matthew! You and I were going to play in the water.

The long letter from Janet, outlining the givens of her

situation, underlined the rather paradoxical state that she found herself in after the recording. It also showed the researchers how a person's overt behaviour is often a poor guide to her philosophy of working. What Janet's children saw of her a good deal of the time (and what we heard on the tape) was 'the person who keeps telling us what's going on, where things are' and so on. What they did not see were the hidden preparations that Janet saw as enabling them free-choice and self-directed activity.

During one recording, Janet spoke to us over the tape to tell us about an event going on in the garden. Two children were fighting over possession of a spade, but Janet refused to get involved.

> Justina is protecting her wheelbarrow and spade and James is trying to encourage Jason to take it away from her . . . Now Jason is trying to discuss the matter with Justina and she's not having any. Peace has been restored. Neither Mrs Russell who is watching from the doorway nor I have become involved in it. Children are playing quite nicely in the sand.

This example illustrates how Janet was often observing her children and actively inhibiting herself from getting involved, taking the view that the children had to work things out for themselves.

Because Janet's overt activity with children missed out on all the givens, the self-restraint and what was going on inside her head as she watched children, it is not surprising that our recordings provided a poor guide to her philosophy. However, the paradox has more important practical implications. When we looked at the reasons why children spontaneously approached Janet, it was nearly always for managerial help – access to turns, equipment, fair play or sympathy. When they came to Rebecca, however, it was usually for interaction – asking her to play, help them make something and so forth (see Appendix B).

What this observation suggested to us was that children, like our recording, saw Janet as a management resource.

There is nothing fundamentally wrong in this, of course, since good management is a vital ingredient in the achievement of educational objectives. However, it did mean that Janet might often be sailing against the wind in trying to find time for her more educationally substantive goals – children were continually pulling her into managerial activity. This suggestion – that supply creates demand – is borne out by our later observations, as we see in the next chapter.

Rebecca was less upset by her recording. She, as we have already seen, produced a quite different tape. She said relatively little over the tape to explain what she was doing and, unlike Janet, she tended to turn the recorder on for long periods and simply leave it going. Her school situation – 'givens' in Janet's terms – was also quite different. Rebecca owned space and activities rather than children. Although she kept the register for a particular group of children and had primary interest in them, there was not the same expectation that she would follow them throughout the school, providing continuous services. Unlike Janet, therefore, Rebecca spent relatively little time searching around or shepherding children. Since she was in close, sustained proximity to equipment like the Wendy house and the painting equipment, she was also likely to be drawn into different activities with children – as we saw in our examination of the reasons why children came to her (Appendix B).

What these observations imply, quite simply, is that the form that interactions between preschoolers and adults take – what type of activity they are involved in; the time available for chat, play and teaching – is intimately bound up with the physical structure of the school and the fit between the school's philosophy and its architectural form. The ideal way forward in our research would have been to supplement our recordings of teachers at work with considerable detailed information about room layout, school design and the general givens of the teacher's day. Janet was clearly right in urging on us the need to look beyond the recordings to such factors, but resources were simply not available for a detailed and systematic study along these lines. However, the whole question of physical constraints, work-sharing and the like remained uppermost in our mind when we came to consider the general implications we might draw from the recordings. We were aware that any personality factors of the teachers and general stylistic qualities in their relationships with children were intimately bound up with their general physical and educational environment.

Language of Preschools

In addition to our exploration of the functions and roles that the two teachers played, we were also interested in the nature of the language used in the groups (for reasons put forward in the last chapter). Initially, we looked at the recordings with a view to establishing the topics and domains of talk – a topic being who or what was being talked about and a domain being the time period involved (the here and now, the past, or future). This line of analysis led us eventually to suggest that there is indeed a language of preschools, a common core of themes and topics which figure regularly in adult–child interactions (Chapter 5). In the following table, we list the proportion of occasions on which Janet's and Rebecca's utterances to their children concerned their past, their here and now, and their future. We also include the timeless domain – this covers talk about the permanent properties of objects (their colour, weight, shape and so forth); the enduring characteristics of people (e.g. mummy always gets happy when I give her a hug) and logical relationships – why wood floats in water, or why pencils break.

	Past	Present	Future	Timeless
Janet	6	75	8	11
Rebecca	4	62	9	25

Table 2.1 *Percentages of conversation by time domain*

The biggest difference lies in Rebecca's much greater involvement in talk about the why's of things, and instruction in number, size, and so forth. Janet's language was more present centred – again, a reflection of her role as manager – of the here-and-now. Not surprisingly, then, the adult's role *vis-à-vis* her children dictates the sort of linguistic environment the children are exposed to. What they gain in practice at thinking about objects, speculating about the future, imaginary things, or considering the past, is a direct manifestation of the tasks and styles adopted by the adults around them. The same argument applies to the topics of conversation, illustrated next.

	Child	Adult	Others	Objects	Miscellaneous
Janet	82	8	0	4	6
Rebecca	58	9	9	9	15

Table 2.2 *Percentages of conversation on particular topics*

The most noticeable feature of this table is Janet's much greater concentration on references to the child himself. Rebecca's pattern is far more varied and includes a good deal of discussion about other people and objects in the environment. Here too, then, management tends to pull language into a rather specific form – concentration on the immediate situation being experienced, about to be experienced, or having just been experienced, by the child himself. This pattern of adult language is reminiscent of that experienced by the child much earlier in his development (Snow and Ferguson, 1977) and, generally, it does little to extend his imagination, knowledge or language in the preschool years.

   In later chapters, we look in more detail at language in the preschool with a view to seeing how far the young child is provided with challenging and stimulating encounters with the adults around him. We try to describe and characterize the nature of conversation with young children – looking at the styles of adult talk and their impact on the part played by the child in interactions. This emphasis on conversation, and particularly the way in which style of management exerts an influence on adult styles, was fostered by the next two practitioners to become involved in this project and, ultimately, in the writing of this book.

Cooperative research – Stage 2

While work with our first two collaborators was in progress, we made our first real contact with the playgroups which, eventually, were to become our main focus. The contact took the form of Yvonne Cranstoun and Linnet McMahon – later to become central members of the team. Linnet McMahon had been involved with the OPRG since its earliest days. She had read of its existence in *Contact*, the magazine of the Pre-School Playgroups Association, and had written to the Director of the project, Jerome Bruner, offering her services. Later, she was to write of her involvement with the project, that it followed on a visit to 'a playgroup with very poor adult–child relationships' which led her to identify the future needs of playgroups in general as:

1 Continue to emphasize the importance of play – free choice among varied activities. This allows more hope of learning, even if adult–child relationships are poor or non-existent, than does an over-controlled, dogmatic, highly structured approach.
2 Teach how to observe children. Skilled observation makes the supervisor's job more interesting.
3 Teach specific child 'management' skills: how to intervene and when; getting down to the child's level; positioning self to have greatest possible overall view.
4 Teach importance of conversation and the 'power of words'.

Linnet McMahon had already participated fully in the child observation work and was to take over shared responsibility for our future contacts with playgroups and nursery schools.

Yvonne Cranstoun came into contact with the group at the in-service meetings. She had shared the feelings of many who attended these gatherings that many of the skills in organizing and running playgroups, like effective, planned management and the provision of opportunities for interesting conversations with children, had not been considered enough by those who ran the proceedings. She had been running a very successful playgroup for some years, and was ideally placed to add the practitioner's voice to our dialogues. She went on to make recordings in the same way that Janet and Rebecca had done.

Yvonne Cranstoun's tape, like Janet's, was also quite high in management activity. She too found this disturbing and not representative of her overall goals or practice. For such an experienced playgroup organizer to have such a marked response to the experience of making tapes was encouraging. She found the analysis interesting and provocative and it led her on to articulate her own goals and techniques more fully: the method clearly had something of value to offer practitioners, then. But Yvonne also brought a note of caution about interpreting the general significance of the analysis. She felt that the recordings did not do justice to the range of activities she involved herself in with the children. Having visited her playgroup and seen things in progress we took her point. It was she who continually kept alive the idea that we might be gaining access in our recordings only to certain aspects of adult style. She went on to make more tapes (see Chapter 8) in which she endeavoured to prove her point. But she also felt that she gained a tremendous amount from listening to the tapes and seeing the transcripts. She felt that the mirror they offered made the practitioner stop and re-examine her practice. For example, she talked about the changing role of the practitioner as she gained experience and moved on from 'helper' role to a more supervising one. This in turn, she pointed out, increased the pressure towards management and threatened to detract attention from more substantive goals – like talking to children. In particular, she found the tape disturbing because management demands were continually overriding her attempts to listen to children and develop ideas with them. In the following extract, Yvonne sets out to talk to children with whom she had not been in contact during the session. However, she tries to do this near a centre of high management demands – the milk table – and the constant demands for management from children persistently disrupt her attempts at extended talk.

Milktime (2)

(aside) There are several children I have not had time to speak to this morning, so I think I will go and supervise dispensing milk. Should give me a chance to have some conversation with them . . .

A: Here we are, then, here's the milk.

CS: (several assertive voices)

A: Would you like to hand me your cup then? Here we are.

C: (Something about red cup).

A: Sorry Natasha? I can't hear you darling. Lee, no more chairs out now please. We have enough. Thank you.

C: Enough.

A: You must wait until someone gets up. We don't have any extra chairs. When someone gets up you can take their place. Now Natasha. You want this yellow one. Right?

C: Is that coke?

c1: I like . . . Coca Cola.

A: No, it's not. There we are. Oh, Rebecca, that was gone very quickly. Lee, there's a space round here if you'd like to come and take Rebecca's place. You are all thirsty this morning, hmm? Had a busy morning.

C: What's in there?

A: Sorry?

C: That.

T: Oh, that one. That's Ribena. James doesn't drink milk, so his mummy brings Ribena. Because he doesn't drink milk. Is that what you thought was coke?

C: Yes.

A: No, no it's not Lee.

c2: Please can I have some?

A: Yes, of course you can. David, did you enjoy doing the Grand Old Duke of York? Hmm? Did you? You all have to practice that a bit more.

c: Do you know Craig?
A: Hello Clare. Yes I know Craig. He goes to school now.
c: (inaudible)
c: But Alan goes to playgroup.
A: Alan still comes to playgroup, yes. But Craig has gone to school, that's right. I'll have to get some more milk in the jug. Just get some down . . . Get one of these bottles here.

Later, Yvonne wrote about this section of her transcript: 'It's evident that very little real conversation was taking place here, just lots of very busy management on my part. Hardly a very productive use of my time with these children . . .'

Yvonne's sentiments – particularly the way in which competing activities led to 'ignoring' children and a failure to develop sustained contacts, was later echoed by a number of other practitioners who took part (Chapter 8). However, as we shall see, Yvonne did not think that the solution to the problem of meeting these many demands lay with a more organized approach to handling children. Adult led, group activities, as we shall see, seldom achieve any real depth in interactions with preschoolers.

This work with the first three participants led to the development of a common language for talking about the job of working with groups of under-fives. It took almost a year. By the time we had gathered equipment, made transcripts, analysed these and discussed them, and then gone on to make new recordings, the nursery and playgroup year were over.

During the following year another 21 practitioners were recruited, 19 playgroup workers and two teachers. The shift of emphasis away from nurseries to playgroups was partly due, no doubt, to the fact that Yvonne Cranstoun's and Linnet McMahon's principal contacts were in the playgroup movement. It was also a reflection of the fact that nursery schools are not very numerous around Oxford. More particularly, however, it reflected a growing concern about the cuts that were looming in the State sector, cuts that eventually culminated in the contraction of nursery provision in the County. The threat introduced by the economic and political climate was hardly conducive to a forward looking, research attitude.

Recruitment of new participants thus shifted mainly to the PPA branches. We now developed techniques not only for recruiting and working with more people, but also for disseminating the findings about different management styles, conversational techniques and so on to groups, using excerpts from our transcripts. This aspect of the work is outlined in Appendix A, together with examples of practice that we used with the group work.

The following chapters report the findings that came out of the work with all 24 participants. How do they vary in style and technique? And how are these differences in style reflected in their relationships with young children?

3

Working in the preschool

When we came to look in detail at the different tasks and activities our 24 practitioners involved themselves in with children, we entertained two quite contradictory notions about what we would find. On the other hand, we had encouraged both teachers and playgroup workers to record only what satisfied them and seemed typical of their own activities. This, we thought, might well lead to totally different types of recordings from one worker to the next. This expectation seemed to be supported by our early reading of the transcripts, which illustrated the tremendous variety of styles that the 24 collaborators brought to their preschool work. On the other hand, we thought it quite feasible that we would find them all doing essentially similar things and performing the same basic functions for children. After all, we knew from previous surveys that preschool workers in general seem to entertain similar goals and objectives (Chapter 1). All 24 preschool groups included children of similar age and provided many of the same materials and opportunities for their children. All this suggested a common pattern of working. What would we find then – practitioners involved in very different basic functions or in very similar ones? And what would be the implications of an affirmative answer to either alternative? These are the questions explored in this chapter.

The initial work with Janet, Rebecca and Yvonne led us to describe the basic tasks they performed for their children in terms of 26 different 'functions'. In the early stages we grouped these together on a purely intuitive basis into five major activities – management, conversation, instruction, play and 'rapport'. The various functions which make up these different activities together with examples of each one are listed in Tables 3.1 to 3.5.

1 *Asks about intention* The adult asks the child what he would like to do next, offering a genuine choice.
'Do you want to paint now, Michael, or later?'
'Do you want to play with the jigsaw next?'

2 *Directs* The child is effectively told what to do next, even where the direction is phrased as a question.
'Story time now, Louise.'
'Do you want to run along to the loo, James?'
'Go and get your coat on, Jenny.'

3 *Prohibits* The adult stops the child from doing something.
'No Mark, you'll hurt Peter.'
'Oh, you are being noisy; that's too noisy a game.'

4 *Negotiates* The adult moves what the children are doing to another place or she delays what they want to do.
'Wait until Darren's finished his painting.'
'That's too noisy a game for in here, why don't you go and play outside?'

5 *Indicates own intention* The adult tells the child what she herself is going to do.
'I'm going to take Peter to the loo.'
'I'll be back in a minute – just going to stop that noise over there.'

6 *Provides services* The adult helps the child to do something preparatory to his own activity.
'Shall I tie your apron, Janie?'
'Let's just do up those shoe laces before you go out.'

Table 3.1 *Management (Working out what to do next)*

7 *Marks action* The adult draws the child's attention to the effects or consequences of his actions.
'If you lean on the Jenny, it'll topple over.'
'Oh, look at the water, you're pouring too fast'.

8 *Describes/highlights environment* The adult draws the child's attention to the objects, events or people to which he should attend.
'Oh, there's some yellow Plasticine you could use.'
'Look at Mark's drawing.'

9 *Asks for description* The adult asks the child to name or comment upon events, objects in the immediate context.
'What colour is that piece, Anne?'
'Which piece do you need next?'

10 *Instructs* The adult tells the child how to do something.
'Why don't you turn that one over?'
'You need to suck much harder to get the water up.'

11 *Assists act* The adult actually helps the child to bring off something he is trying to do.
'If we just make a hole in there . . . and then push this through, there!'

12 *Demonstrates* The adult actually shows the child how to do something.
'Watch: first you have to put this one, and then that fits.'

13 *Evaluates* The adult passes some comment on the status of what the child has just done or made.
'Oh, that's lovely, Jamie.'
'There – you are a big girl.'

14 *Asks for evaluation* The adult asks the child to evaluate his own product.
'Do you think that looks quite right, Stephen?'

Table 3.2 *Instruction (Establishing how to do what we're already doing)*

15 *Elaborates pretend symbolic play* The adult extends the child's play theme.
'Oh, and you're the big wolf – come to eat me up.'
'You're the nurse – are you going to bandage my poorly leg?'

16 *Acts as spokesman for rules of the game*
'Nurses don't lie in bed – patients do.'
'Oh, we need knives and forks if we're going to have dinner.'

17 *Allocates roles*
'You be the policeman, Jamie.'
'You lay the table, Melissa.'

Table 3.3 *Pretend play*

18 *Asks for information* The adult asks the child a question about events not ongoing.
'What did you do at the seaside, Peter?'
'Did you go to the shops with Mummy?'

19 *Gives information* The adult tells the child something about events not ongoing.
'We had the photographer in last week.'
'There was a mouse in playgroup yesterday.'

20 *Asks for causal explanation* The adult goes beyond appearance of events to talk about 'why'.
'Why do you think those big men won't fit in there?'
'Why does that always fall off?'

21 *Gives causal explanation*
'That won't make a noise because you didn't wind it up yet.'

22 *Talks about reasons for others' actions* The adult talks about why people act as they do.
'Mummy will be very upset, because she left her keys.'
'Poor Jamie, he's crying 'cause he hurt his knee.'

Table 3.4 *Conversation*

23 *Agrees with child*
'Yes, that is the one we had last week.'
'John has gone to big school, yes.'

24 *Disagrees with child*
'No, today is Thursday, not Wednesday.'

25 *Repeats what the child has just said* Verbatim or paraphrased repetition.
'Oh, mummy went to the hairdresser?'
'You are going on three holidays.'

26 *Monitors* The adult makes some comment or utterance that acknowledges what the child has said, but does not add anything.
'Lovely!'
'Super!'
'You are lucky!'

Table 3.5 *Rapport*

Once we had transcribed each of the 24 opening, 'documentary' tapes from the practitioners, we classified each adult move towards children into the 26 categories just listed. Detailed examples are given in Appendix B. What were we to find, then? Little or no similarity between practitioners in what they did with children, or a marked pattern of agreement?

We found a good deal of agreement. It seemed that the task of working with groups of preschool children led on to a common core pattern of activities which transcends the differences in adult styles. However, while marked and interesting, this common pattern only held over approximately half the functions identified. There was a set of tasks that all adults were involved in quite frequently and others which they seldom took on. But the middle ground activities – those that happened a good deal on some tapes, but seldom on others – were also quite extensive. What, then, do adults generally do in common in the service of their groups of preschoolers and where do the major differences between them lie?

In Table 3.6 the different functions are listed again, this time showing their order of popularity in the recordings.

Function	Rank sum	Rank range
Monitors	79·5	1–10
Asks for information	84·0	1–11
Repeats what child has said	93·0	1–15
Describes/highlights environment	115·5	1–11·5
Gives information	134·5	2–13
Directs	179·0	1–13·5
Asks for description	180·5	2·5–21
Agrees with child	194·0	4–18
Instructs	218·0	1–21
Evaluates	287·5	5–22
Marks action	316·5	4–23
Asks about intention	324·5	4–22
Negotiates	353·5	8·5–23·5
Elaborates pretend play	358·0	1–23
Gives causal explanation	392·0	6–23
Indicates own intention	393·0	7–24
Prohibits	406·0	7–23
Assists act	413·0	8–33·5
Demonstrates	443·5	9–24
Disagrees with child	464·5	10–24·5
Provides services	473·5	14–24
Asks for evaluation	475·0	13·5–24
Talks about reasons for actions	495·5	8·5–24
Allocates roles	495·5	11·5–24·5
Acts as spokesman for rules	513·0	11·5–24
Asks for causal explanation	514·5	13–26

Table 3.6 *Popularity of functions*

Statistical note*

The simplest way to discuss the list of functions shown in Table 3.6 is to consider them in three groups. The first six functions listed occur in the top half of every practitioner's list of activities and all but 'gives information' occur at the top of at least one individual's list. In other words, these six

*See Appendix 2 for all statistical comparisons

activities are relatively frequent in every playgroup worker's and nursery teacher's interactions with her children. A similar pattern occurs at the bottom of the list, where the last six functions almost always occur in the bottom half of every practitioner's list and every single one appears as the (tied) least frequent activity on one or more lists. In other words, these interactions did not appear frequently in any of the recordings.

As we move towards the middle of the list a quite different pattern emerges. Consider *elaborates pretend play* and *instructs* for example. These are the activities which set one practitioner off from another most clearly. On one tape, for example, involvement in pretend play was that playgroup worker's most frequent activity – accounting for 73 per cent of her interactions with children. Against this, not one pretend play interaction occurred on 14 of the recordings. A similar but less dramatic pattern occurs for *instructs*.

By looking in some detail at the popular, unpopular and optional activities found in the recordings we begin to get some insights into the common demands of preschool care, into practitioners' philosophies about what they should and should not do with their charges, and some insights into the differences in approach and style, from adult to adult.

Popular activities

Two of the most frequent and popular moves of adult towards child are part of what we termed the 'rapport' dimension—*monitors* and *repeats what child has just said.* Monitoring, recall, is an utterance from the adult which let the child know she was there but which did not directly provoke any response or activity from him. The following is an example:

c: I'm going to play with the cars.
a: Oh, lovely.
c: And I . . . I'm going to do my painting.
a: Super.

The frequency with which the adult repeats what the child says (perhaps in a paraphrased form) surprised us initially. It is, in fact, the third most frequent form of adult move. It is probably a device for letting the child know that he is being listened to and understood.

Other researchers, notably Tizard *et al.*, have drawn attention to the frequency of these utterances in the speech of nursery school teachers. Partly, they too regard them as rapport – what they term 'social oil', or keeping the wheels of adult–child interactions in motion. They also point out, however, that there is often a more negative side to this type of utterance. They are often used, in effect, to fend off children – as a device for not getting involved with them:

> A: What did you do at the seaside with your daddy?
> c: I buried him in the sand.
> c1: I'm making sand castles.
> A: Wow! And did you leave your daddy in the sand?

The 'Wow!' in the last utterance acknowledges c1's offering, but effectively fends him off while the adult maintains her dialogue with the first child.

> c: I can't do this hard one.
> A: Oh dear.
> c: Will you do it with me?
> A: Oh, you can do it. You're a big girl now.

Here the 'Oh dear' seems to be just a way of acknowledging the child, while not getting involved in her efforts and the jigsaw. The follow up confirms this interpretation.

In the chapter on the structure of conversations we look in much greater detail at these features of practitioner discourse to illustrate their rather double-edged nature. Sometimes monitoring and repeating play a vital role in sustained, interesting talk and instruction with preschoolers. At other times, they are effectively ways of preventing interaction.

Rapport moves, then, may be interactive or noninteractive. They serve both as conversational devices and as management ploys for keeping children out of an adult's hair. It is the context in which they occur, the way in which they dovetail or fail to dovetail with the child's interests and intentions, that marks them as one activity or the other.

Also in the popular list is the category, *directs*. Management thus figures prominently in most recordings. The type of management involved varies considerably, however. 'Directions' take on a variety of styles which, like rapport, depend upon the way that they intrude on the child's ongoing interests. Some managerial activity is enabling. Rebecca, for example, occasionally managed children's activity, but this was usually in response to requests from the children to participate in or initiate some activity. In other words, her control over their actions on the recording was usually taken in the service of the children's own stated intentions. In the following extract, we see how Rebecca was concerned with establishing the conditions – equipment, seating and layout – under which the children could see through their own activities.

> c: Can I do it too?
> A: Well you can come too, Katy, would you like to do some? If you can get right round that table and go and sit down in those two chairs. . . . No, you'll have to go the other way. Owen, right round that way.
> c3: I'm I think I'll do mine in one minute.
> A: . . . that's it, bring a chair.
> c: That's very quickly.
> A: I should take all these off. Can you move over so that Katy can sit down, Owen?
> A: No, Daniel, you sit here, love.
> c: Which chair?
> A: Just there, then Katy and Owen can sit in these two. Right now, can you just reach that one for me? Hello, hello baby.
> c: I'm going home.

A: Remember what we said about this?
c: Yes.
A: What's special about it, Katy?
c: That's the (symmetrical ?) one . . .

Other control encounters were quite different in nature. Some, which we called 'crisis' management, were called out by potential danger or conflict. The adult responds to the inherent threats involved in playgroup activities – a seesaw which poses a threat to fingers, or a cooking session with its encumbent risk of burns. In these cases, the presence of a number of children, often in a boistrous frame of mind, leads to an abandonment of the principle of letting children work freely – for obvious reasons.

On the seesaw
c: It's balanced.
c: It's balanced now.
A: Oh, has it? We'll have a go in a minute, Libby.
c: Can I have a go now?
A: In a minute, yes.
c: Two more to get on it right now.
A: A bit. I think if you put two more on, you're going to have problems – because you might catch your fingers. You're getting your fingers very close to the middle there.
c: Standing inside!
A: That's it – you get on there now. I'll hold your dog. But mind your fingers, Samantha.
c: No it's too much.
A: You'd better get off, Charlotte or Cathy.
c: Mind your fingers, Charlotte.
c: Cathy, you can have this . . .
c1: Can I have that picture?
c2: Can I now?
A: That's it, Move down a little bit. Move back this way.
A: Mind your fingers!

c: She's pushing!

A: Don't push Charlotte any more towards the middle and I'll . . . or you'll squash your fingers.

These forms of management encounter are inevitable where resources are in short supply and long demand; where the interests of several children have to be woven into a mutually satisfying pattern and where a potentially dangerous activity is seen as a necessary and useful feature of preschool experience. Another style of management, however, seems to rest much more on the organization of the particular group in question. This we have termed 'directive management'. It is illustrated in the following extracts:

Going-out time

A: Rachael, time to go out. Get your wellies on, love. John, time to go out. Put away the trains and get your wellies. All together, over here. Come on, John. Right children, fingers on lips. Fingers on lips. Shh . . . Yes, you're very clever talking with your fingers on your lips like that. But shh . . . Peter, wellies on, good boy. Fingers on lips. (chorus of shh . . .)

Even where the adult is actively directing children's activities, then, the extent to which she is imposing external, and, for the children, arbitrary, demands varies fundamentally. As with rapport, what differentiates one form or style of managing from another is the extent to which the adult's move is contingent upon the child's own, ongoing behaviour. Where there is a clear continuity between management and the children's intentions, then it is obviously child-centred. Where it is not, it may well appear arbitrary and unfair. Even when it is in the best interests of the child – as in a dangerous activity – it may not be seen by the child as an integral part of his needs and wishes. To the extent that danger intrudes or timetabled demands exist, this conflict between the immediate intentions of the child and the will imposed by the adult will be an inevitable and endemic part of adult–child relationships. To the extent that such conflicts can be minimized by good planning, then the management which is left can be more responsive to the children's needs.

Also in the list of popular functions are adult moves which are predominantly educational in nature. *Asks for information* includes those encounters between adult and child in which the child is asked to tell the adult something to which he, but not she, is privy. For example, he may be asked about his holidays, where he went at the weekend, who he has just been playing with and so forth. The mirror image of this category, *gives information*, is also in the list of top functions. Here, the teacher might be telling the child something about her own ideas and opinions. A good deal of this sort of talk, however, has to do indirectly with management – when the teacher tells the child when storytime is, where to get his milk from and so forth.

Describes/highlights environment is another popular form of giving information. Unlike asking for information, however, this concerns descriptions of the immediate here-and-now, what the child is looking at, doing, or working with, for example. Such language is highly context specific, and concerned predominantly with rather mundane vocabulary to do with the colour and names of things. We discuss this fully in Chapter 5, 'The language of the preschool'.

In the top list of functions, then, we find a mixture of conversation, management and rapport functions that is characteristic of all our early recordings. Note that there is nothing on play, little to do with the shared doing or making of things and nothing by way of logical reasoning or causal thinking in this list. The language used, as we see in Chapter 5, is usually the language of management and description, with an element of conversation about events and happenings outside the immediate environment.

Unpopular activities

The more demanding, intellectual uses of language – why do things work as they do, what makes people tick, why do they do what they do and so forth, are extremely rare. Where they do occur, as we shall see in Chapter 5, it is usually in response to quite specific topics of conversation – notably about home and hearth.

The low incidence is open to several different explanations. It may be that young children are uninterested in or incapable of talking about these matters. Teachers and playgroup workers thus naturally steer away from them. Maybe the children are only capable of rather mundane talk about the here-and-now. Alternatively, the explanation might lie with the adult and her philosophy or condition. Perhaps she has not the time or inclination to get involved with children in what would have to be extended and demanding interactions. The structure of the preschool, with its range of activities and groups of children may simply not permit adults to work closely enough with children to challenge and extend them into thought-provoking exchanges. Clearly, this aspect of adult–child relationships is crucial from the point of view of the child's development – particularly where he is in all-day care. If the environmental demands are set too low for his developing interests and ability, time and opportunities are being lost.

If the problem lies with numbers and noise, then a solution must be looked for in terms of more adult resources and a more sympathetic environment. We will argue in the following pages that the child often produces his most competent performances when he is alone with the adult or with her as part of a small group of three. We shall investigate the reasons for this and ask how far the absence of sustained, adult–child interactions on a one-to-one basis accounts for the rather context-dependent nature of much preschool language. In Chapter 8 we also see if adults are willing and able to modify their situation or their styles, or both, to encourage more extensive interactions with their children.

This should give us some insights into the basis for context dependency – does it lie with the child, the practitioner or the situation?

Optional activities

In many respects, the set of optional activities are the most interesting, in that they help us to etch out the different working roles that adults perform in the preschool. The common elements just considered give us insights both into what may be the inevitable aspects of work with groups of children and those activities which are largely ruled out by the adults' philosophies or children's nature. But the middle range of categories helps us to understand some of the reasons why the 24 recordings appear so different from each other. All major roles appear in the centre list – management (*negotiates, prohibits, asks about intention, indicates own intention*) practical instruction, where adult and child share the doing, making or understanding of something (*instructs, evaluates, marks act, demonstrates, gives causal explanation*) and play (*elaborates pretend play*).

When we add together all the activities that each adult is involved in under the headings listed in Tables 3.1 to 3.5 – management, instruction, pretend play, conversation, and rapport – the differences between practitioners and their preschool roles are highlighted. Some act basically as managers, others as playmates; some act as teachers while others are basically conversationalists. Rapport tends to transcend all activities. Monitoring and repetition occur frequently in play, conversation, management and instruction.

Overall, direct management accounted for 10 per cent of all interactions, and to these we must add the more subtle conversational moves in management, like *monitoring*, which often takes on a managerial function. Play is the least popular activity, accounting for only 6 per cent of involvement. Conversation, rapport and practical instruction take almost equal shares of the remaining 84 per cent interactions.

But these averages mask the marked individual differences already mentioned. Management on some tapes occupies less than 5 per cent of adult activity, on others it rises to 44 per cent. Play and instruction, as we have seen, vary widely, some adults spending more than three quarters of their tape time in play, others showing not a single play encounter. Conversation, like rapport, is more equally distributed.

Do these differences matter? What do the children get from the different interactions, and how do they influence the general levels of competence they display in their dealings with adults? This is the question we look at in most detail in the next chapter, and we take it up again in Chapters 6 and 7. The short answer is that the differences do matter, a great deal.

In fact, the effect of the framework set by the adult, and the style of control that she brings to bear in working with young children, is enormous. Some adults are involved with children in interesting, unusual, egalitarian activities – play, instruction and conversation. Others, despite similar investment of time and effort, fail to achieve those, and their interactions are either extremely adult-dominated or rather disjointed and sporadic. In part, we believe that these differences are due to philosophy and environmental conditions – the way in which work is shared out by adults in the group, the room lay-out and the other factors we have touched upon. But the styles may also reflect the adult's basic personality and approach to children.

One of the first indices to suggest that different adults might well be being perceived in different ways by children, as we saw in Chapter 2, was the result of an examination of the reasons why they initiated contact with adults. We wondered whether adults who managed a good deal were also approached for management, while those who interacted with children in talk, play and making things were approached more often for personal interactions. This difference had shown through in children's overtures to Janet and Rebecca but would it hold over the 24 practitioners as a group? It did. Generally speaking, management seemed to breed more management, interactions more interactions. Where an adult herself usually initiated contact with children for purposes of management, children often came to her for similar purposes. Their spontaneous overtures took the form of requests for turns and arbitration; questions about when storytime was and other basically managerial functions. However, where the adult was holding a conversation with children or playing with them, the opening from a 'new' child was much more likely to be a request for her to play with them, help them do something or simply to talk.

In the next chapter we see how children often jump in to conversations taking place between an adult and other children. These would be classified as interaction openings – the child is looking for some involvement with the adult, not simply using her as an avenue to turns and equipment. When we looked, then, at the proportion of adult opening moves towards children which were concerned with management rather than extended personal interaction, and then did the same for children's openings towards them, we found a significant correlation (Appendix B).

The major implication of this result is that supply creates demand. The adult may have many goals and objectives – may be actively creating conditions under which children can follow their own noses and so forth. But our findings suggest that where her main contacts with children are managerial they tend to categorize her as the one to be approached for management. What she supplies, children come to demand of her. Again, this suggests that once in a cycle of active management, the adult is pulled deeper and deeper into managerial action by the children themselves. There is nothing fundamentally wrong in this of course. At best, the adult who manages frees other practitioners in the group to take part in extended personal interactions, conversation, instruction and play. However, the fact that they may be creating conditions under which they are increasingly likely to manage, may well be unsatisfactory to the adults in question. That is what we generally found in talking over tapes with 'high managers'.

Our discussions with practitioners often revolved around this subject of management. What is it, we asked, that leads some adults into a good deal of control over children's activities, sometimes to the extent of destroying their attempts at other activities with their children? Consider the paradox, for example, of a trained teacher faced with a group of children and armed with a solitary assistant. The task of management falls, perhaps naturally, on her shoulders. As senior member of the team, the trained and qualified one, it is perhaps inevitable that she should take on the role of organizer. At the same time, however, her training in teaching children, helping them develop and understand, is put at risk by this push towards management. There were a number of episodes, like the following, which illustrated the dilemma. Here the teacher was trying to draw children into the scheduled activity, but in so doing she threatened to disrupt the activity of one child who had just managed to get hold of a much-sought-after toy and has started playing with it. Here it is the assistant who has been observing the child and who steps in to act as spokesman for him. The teacher could not know what trouble and patience he had shown in gaining access to the toy.

A: Milk time, milk time children. Damion, have you had your milk?

C: (quietly) No.

A: Go and get your milk then, love.

C: Ohh . . .

A1: He's only just got those cars, been waiting for ages to get them.

A: Oh . . . well, play for a little while, but then you have to get your milk.

Management, which at best holds all the more substantive goals and materials together, can become the adult's primary activity. She may, unknowingly, occupy close to half her time directing children. The various factors – situational, philosophical and personal – which interact to produce the very high incidences of crises and directive management, deserve much fuller study and research. In the remainder of this short book, however, the whole question of effective management of resources fades into the background as we focus in on the ways in which adults control children in conversation, play and teaching encounters. The word 'control' is central to our descriptions and discussions of adult–child interactions. Although it is a word which might, on first sight, seem rather at variance with the child-centred aspirations and methods of preschool practitioners, we choose it deliberately to underline the fact that however child-centred the adult, the fact remains that the locus of control in verbal and physical interactions with children is very much in her hands.

Some conversations, play episodes and instructional sessions between adult and child are extremely adult-dominated. Some adults, by questions and directions, establish and maintain the course of their encounters with children themselves. Reading such transcripts, one is never in doubt as to who is adult and who is the child; the adult is very much in the driving seat. Other recordings show little genuine interaction with children at all: the adult maintains a 'distance' between the children's activities and her own. Encounters with children are almost invariably short, involving few turns in either talk or shared action. Often, this shortness results from the managerial intention of the adult, but at other times it seems to result from a more self-conscious decision of hers not to get enmeshed with children, perhaps made from fear that adult control might inhibit or destroy the integrity of the children's learning and development. However, such apparent lack of control exercises in reality another, more subtle form of control over the course of children's experiences, as we shall see. Children respond systematically to adults in such a way that the course and direction of their interactions lie much more in the adult's hands than they do the child's. Thus, whatever the child gains or fails to gain from his contacts with the adult remains very much her responsibility.

Some adults manage to help create encounters with children in which there is a genuine sharing of control – where, for example, the child asks the adult questions, thus controlling the course of a conversation, or where he tells her what to do in order that they might bring off some difficult enterprise together. Children may thus adopt an imperative tone – 'look!' 'watch!' 'look at this!' – controlling the adult's attention and, hence her experiences. In such encounters as these, if we rub off the 'Cs' and 'As' on the transcripts, and get rid of the odd phrase like 'my mummy', we actually lose sight of who is adult and who is child. No doubt, children have to be at a certain level of competence and confidence to bring off these encounters, but we shall try to show in the following pages that it is largely the adult who supplies or fails to supply a framework or situation in which children will be able to show off such levels of confidence and competence.

We start, in the next chapter, with an examination of different styles of conversation. This, in fact, is our 'strongest' data, since conversation occurs so frequently on our recordings. For purposes of analysis, it also relies less than play or instruction upon a detailed knowledge of context and non-verbal behaviour. How, then, do practitioners go about the task of talking to young children?

4

Conversations with the preschool child

Holding interesting and stimulating conversations with pre-school children is no easy task. For a child, reliving his experiences, or revealing his thoughts and feelings for the benefit of a relative stranger, stretches his abilities and often his listener's to the limit. Because there is no natural, automatic way to guarantee good two-way communication with young children, when we come to look carefully at the approaches that our group of teachers and playgroup work-ers bring to the task, it will come as no surprise to find, as we do, a great variety of styles.

The main purpose of this chapter is to describe and illustrate the various styles of adult conversation and, in detail, to work out some of the effects that they might have on the language and experience of the children involved. We will, at the same time, also gain some insights into the preschool child's conversational abilities – uncovering aspects of the skills needed to hold extended dialogues, which create particular difficulties for young children. Those insights into children's language ability help us to understand why animated and interesting talk with them is so difficult to achieve, and so help us understand why different practition-ers act in the way they do.

Our main proposition is that the various styles of conversa-tion that adults bring into the classroom and playgroup exert a tremendous influence upon the children's part in and contribution to talk, and, indeed, represent one of the main factors which determine how well a child plays his part as a conversationalist. Some adults manage to get children asking a relatively large number of questions, encourage them to elaborate freely in their responses to their questions and, in general, prompt them to play active, productive roles in dialogue. Others are much more likely to receive only monosyllabic, terse and somewhat reluctant offerings from children, despite a similar investment of time, effort and dedication. Why?

These general differences in style and effect are suggested both by an intuitive examination of the transcripts (some of which we present in this chapter) and a more exhaustive, formal analysis of conversations.

Some of the differences in adult style that we shall be considering may well have been influenced by the fact that the conversations were deliberately recorded for research purposes, and thus may not be absolutely typical of everyday styles. This point will be taken up and discussed more fully in Chapter 8. They might also be due to differences between the children: some children, for example, may demand more questions to keep them involved in conversations than others do. However, we shall present evidence which suggests strongly that children's relative contributions to conversations and the ease and fluency with which they play their parts, reside to a great extent in the adult's hands. The way a child makes use of an adult as a talking resource depends very largely upon the way that the adult presents herself to him in conversation.

Why study conversation?

Encouraging children to talk about their ideas, experiences and feelings was seen by our practitioners as one of their principle contributions to those children's overall development. Indeed, of the 24 who made documentary tapes for us, 16 elected to make further, experimental tapes in which they took conversation as their primary focus of interest.

However, in spite of the preference for dialogue in our later recordings, and the belief of both practitioners and psychologists in its importance to the child, we know surprisingly little about its nature. The little work that has been done – particularly that of Barbara Tizard and her colleagues – suggests that much of the dialogue between adult and child takes place at too low a level, relatively, to be likely to exert any really positive influence on a child's linguistic, social or mental growth.

There is, however, a considerable body of literature about the nature of the language used between parents and children aged up to about two years (e.g. Snow and Ferguson, 1977). This work underlines the tremendous natural ability that parents bring to bear in understanding their children and talking to them at an appropriate level. However, as the children grow, become more imaginative, capable of remembering distant events and thinking verbally, a much greater demand is placed on both their language and on their listeners' abilities. Talking to children in the preschool situation is quite a different affair from the parent–child dialogue of early development. As we shall see, there is no natural ability ensuring that all adults handle the demands of conversation effectively.

Conversations with young children, at best, give one insights into their needs, ideas, feelings, fears and attitudes. They are a primary basis for reaching an understanding of each child. Conversations with an interested and sensitive adult give a child an opportunity to relive memorable experiences, to find out about the needs and feelings of others, to hear new and exciting things and to discover the interest that his ideas have for others. In putting language to work in the service of others, he develops his own power to think in words and to express what he feels and knows clearly. At best, that is. But often the best is not forthcoming.

Insensitive, pre-planned, deliberate attempts by adults to provide children with the benefits of conversation on a scheduled basis can be far from satisfying, as the following rather pointed tale from Tom Crabtree in the *Guardian* illustrates.

The playgroup leader, bless her, enthused by hearing about language programmes, addressed the crew thus:

'Now children, we're all going to talk.' A forest of hands went up of under-fives wanting to go to the toilet. One child muttered loudly: 'Oh bugger. Talking-time again.' Another child was whispering something to me about a pound note he'd lost that weekend, his uncle had given it to him as a joke, and he'd run out to the sweetshop with it, but it had fallen out of his hand and the wind had blown it away . . . 'Stop talking, Vernon,' said the lady. 'Now children, I want us all to look at this picture of a house . . .'

Conversation demands a blend of talking and listening. As we shall see, listening tends to be the difficult part. True conversations are not too staged-managed; they come about by a genuine desire of two or more people to explore each others thoughts and feelings. Children, as we will show, are by no means insensitive to the requirements for proper conversations and, as the Crabtree tale illustrates, adults ignore this sophistication at their peril.

Before going on to look in detail at different conversational styles and their departures from natural conversation, however, we need to look briefly at some aspects of the preschool child's level of conversational ability. This will help us to understand some of the problems that practitioners face in talking to him and give us some insights into how their different styles originate.

Framing and chaining

One very dominant feature of young children's language which we observed many times in our recordings was the rather pre-emptive way in which they would jump in when others were already talking. How far this lack of 'framing', as we called it, was due to their poor working knowledge about the etiquette of group talk, or how far to the child-centred atmosphere in which they were seldom admonished for any signs of initiative, we cannot say. However, whatever the reason for this feature of their conversation, it often presented considerable problems for the adult, particularly in combination with another rather charming feature of the way children attend to and get involved in the conversation of others. This second characteristic we called 'chaining', acknowledging the link between our observations and those made by the Soviet psychologist, Vygotsky (1936), who first drew our attention to this characteristic of children's thinking.

Perhaps the best way to describe these two aspects of child talk is through a series of examples drawn from our recordings. Look out for the way in which children often enter a dialogue without framing their entries with pleasantries like 'That reminds me . . .', 'It's funny you should say that . . .,' 'Oh, Mrs Russell . . .,' and so on. Note too the way in which different children come into the conversation by picking up some aspect of what has been said and elaborating on it, so that successive moves from different children read rather like a chain, each move attached by one link to the next. In the first example, the basis for the links is clearly transport.

Getting about

A: Have you ever been on a boat before, Mark?
c1: Ah . . . No.
A: Are you looking forward to going?
c1: Hmm.
A: Have you ever been in an aeroplane?
c1: No . . . but . . .
c2: (interrupts) I've been in . . . in a bus.
A: A bus?
c2: Yes . . . 'cause I've . . . our car broke down, so we had to . . . 'cause dad couldn't do it . . . make it go again, so we had to . . . hmm . . . (inaudible).
A: Do you know how to get your car on the boat?
c3: Drive it.
A: Oh, Daddy's going to drive it on.
c3: Hmm.
A: Does mummy drive?

c3: No.

A: Doesn't she?

c3: Can't.

A: Oh, she can't.

c4: My . . . my mummy wants to drive Daddy's car but she can't, 'cause Daddy keeps moaning!

c5: And, my mummy can ride a bike, and last time she ride a bike all the way to Wantage!

A: Did she?

A: I bet that was hard work.

c1: Mine wouldn't even let . . . wouldn't even do it, 'cause she hasn't even got a bike.

A: She hasn't got a what? . . . a bike?

c1: No.

A: Oh dear.

c2: My mummy has.

A: Has she?

c2: Yes.

A: Do you go on the back of your mummy's bike? (pause) No?

c3: I do.

c: One time when mummy was trying to ride it, she fell off the bike and hurt, started . . . she fell down and all the blood falled out of it.

This transcript, and the next to follow, suggest that the young children involved are intuitively thinking in superordinate categories. One speaker mentions boats, say, and this leads another to talk about cars or aeroplanes; the children are clearly capable, then, of intuitively classifying different 'modes of getting about' under the same general theme or heading, and this frequently underlies the chaining found in their conversations.

Accidents

c1: We . . . we had to go . . . down to the sea, and daddy walked down, and we . . . I slipped down on my bum and so did daddy . . . and . . . 'cause there was too much (wet?) on there.

A: Oh I know, and made it slippery.
c1: Yeh . . . then we . . . eat on our blankets and we
    went to the sea.
c2: And . . . when Brian came last . . . a . . . we did
    go . . . when it was out . . . when it was
    Christmas . . . a . . . we . . . Graham sat on a
    swing and swinged and he skidded off.
A: Did he?
c2: He skidded onto the ground.

Not all the chaining is due to such relatively sophisticated
linking of different ideas through general themes, however.
Sometimes children seem to pick up on part of the utterance
which specifies a relationship, like 'I got . . .' and quite
different content areas, such as 'I got an auntie' and 'I got
new shoes' follow on each other, chained by the shared idea
of possession. At other times, children chain at the word
level or even at the phonetic level, so that one word triggers
another of quite different meaning but with a similar sound,
as in the first of the following examples.

Nanar's Nanas
    c1: There's bananas.
    A: Bananas. Do you like bananas?
    c: (and several others chorus) Yes.
    c1: I like nanas, I like nanas.
    A: Do you like bananas?
    c1: Yes.
        (Other children speak at same time about bananas.)
    c2: I've got two nanars and two grandads.
    A: Two nannies, and two grandads have you? You're
        very lucky.
    c: They're, they like nanas.
    A: Oh, who else has got two Nannies and two Gran-
        dads?
    c: I have, I have.

I'm going . . . and the size of things
c1: I'm going to Clare's.
A: Are you, that'll be nice, won't it?
c2: I'm going to my Nana's this week.
A: Are you? Where?
  You're going there tomorrow? Oh you are lucky aren't you?
c: And I'm going . . . I'm going to big school.
A: Are you?
c2: I'm going to school.
A: When is that?
c2: (inaudible)
A: Next Tuesday, right.
c: Look what I did.
A: Oh, that's tiny isn't it?
c: Yes.
c1: My nan's got a little big nose.
A: A little big nose.

Sickness in the family
A: And is mummy feeling better now?
c: And I am.
A: And you are too, yes.
c1: I help my mummy every morning.
A: Do you? That's lovely.
c2: My mums gone, my baby's gone too . . .
c1: (at same time) My, when, when I was sick . . .
A: Your baby's?
c1: (continues) . . . I was sick, then I, Mummy wouldn't let me go in the garden, then I was sick.
A: Oh dear.
c1: I couldn't come to play school could I?
A: No you couldn't, if you were sick, could you?
c1: No.
A: No, you had to. Well, you wouldn't have wanted to come (c: No) would you, if you didn't feel very well (c: No) No.
c2: And I was sick. I got it on my sock.

Carpets

A: Oh, well, when I was a little girl if I lost a tooth the fairies used to leave me a . . . sixpence, under the carpet . . . to pay for my bad tooth.

c1: We . . . we're getting a new carpet soon.

A: Are you? Lucky you . . . that's very nice.

c1: Oh my baby's crying . . . good-bye.

A death in the family

A: Is she your auntie?

c: No.

A: No?

c1: I've got a auntie.

A: You've got a auntie, have you? . . . who's your auntie?

c1: I have now.

A: Oh, what's her name. Can you remember?

c1: Auntie.

A: Just Auntie? Oh that's nice isn't it?

c1: Yes.

c: 'Cept my Auntie's gone to heaven.

A: Has she?

c: Yes. 'Cept on Sunday, Nanny went up to heaven.

A: Did they?

c: Yes.

A: Gone to live with the angels did they?

c1: My mummy went to the shop yesterday and she bought me some sweets.

A: Oh that's nice. What sort were they?

In these different conversations, children were motivated to talk by what they overheard between two other people, and as we pointed out above, they do not usually announce the fact that they intend to join in, nor, so far as we can tell, do they wait for the conversation to pause. However, they do not always neglect to frame their conversational entries. In fact, we got the impression from our tapes that this ability or knowledge was just developing in young children – perhaps, indeed, pushed on by their experience as conversationalists in the preschool itself. In the following, quite amusing example, note how the little boy not only gains the attention of his teacher before giving her his main message, he actually seems to lay a verbal trap for her.

A: What are you going to do, Lisa?
c: Paint.
c1: Guess what I'm going to do, Mrs Russell
A: What?
c1: Nothing!

A similar feature is less humourously represented in the following transcripts too. These represent quite important linguistic, social and intellectual developments in children. They are not simply putting their ideas straight into words, but preparing the ears of their listeners before they do so, deferring their immediate wish – to tell someone something – until they have alerted that person to their intention to speak. In view of the rather impulsive nature of young children, the relatively free and easy atmosphere of the preschool, and the considerable social maturity involved in framing, it's no surprise to find that most of the preschoolers, most of the time, do not do it.

c: I want to tell you about my hunting now Suzy. Do you know what?
c1: What?
c: You know, you know what my horse did yesterday?
c2: Can I tell you something? I've got Tipstick.
A: Got Tipstick, have you?

The conversational styles of preschool adults

The rather impulsive quality of many children's entry into conversation, together with their tendency to pick up on an ongoing chat and 'chain' in the way we have seen, prove to be major obstacles in the way of truly sustained, elaborated conversations between child and adult – particularly where there are a number of children in earshot.

Some adults are extremely responsive to children's openings, to the extent that they seldom ignore what a child says even when they have just asked another a question which has yet to be answered, as in the following transcript.

Pets

c: I've got a birdie.

A: You've got a birdie, and what's his name.

c2: I gotta birdie.

A: Jake?

c2: And my cat's name is Ginger.

A: Your cat's Ginger. What's yours . . .

c: Er, Cocoa,

A: Cocoa.

c2: (breaks in) Do you like my shirt.

A: That's a lovely shirt, isn't it

c2: I've got two . . .

c: (at same time) I've got one.

c: (at same time) And yesterday . . . bone up to his (?)

c1: Have you got a dog?

A: And who's that, your dog?

c: I've got this dress on.

A: That's a very nice dress.

c2: (interrupts) A bird (?) like dress . . .

A: Yes it's a pretty dress. Is that the dress you had on for your photos. Is it. And what's Mummy done with your photo?

c: She tooked it home.

A: Did she? Did she put it on the shelf for people to see?

c1: I went with my mummy in Scotland with Farnborough, the seaside.

If the teacher or playgroup worker is going to acknowledge every opening from a group of children, then interactions with each child will seldom extend beyond two or three moves. No idea or experience is going to be elaborated in any depth and the whole course of adult–child talk will take on a rather disjointed, superficial quality, as in the next episode.

Colours

c1: A red, a red, a red
c2: Red what?
A: Where's red? You haven't got any red on today have you? Hm?
c: This is red.
A: That's right, that's right, yes, good.
c1: I've got two reds on.
A: Mm.
c3: I've got red.
c4: I haven't got any red on at all.
A: No you haven't have you.
c1: I have.
A: You have, yes. Where have you got red?
c1: Here.
c3: I got red here.
A: On your jumper.
c2: I got red.
A: Well, yes you have, yes.
c3: I've got some red.
    (several voices talking about 'red')
c: I've got blue and red on.
A: Blue yes. Has anyone else got blue on.
c: I have. (several other voices: I have, I have, I have got blue.)
c?: Do you know what colour's my ...?
c: Shut up.
A: That's a lot of noise.
c: I got red.

This style of adult conversation, in which the adult is generally pulled this way and that as she seeks to attend to all children's initiatives, we called 'floating'. Although it appears periodically in the transcripts, however, it was not a dominant style of adult response. In general, adult questions far out-number children's – though the degree of imbalance varies substantially from one practitioner to another. And, generally speaking, most of the adults we worked with did not simply allow their questions to die away; they would usually follow through on their questions and on other conversational moves so that where another child attempted to chime in, they would fend him off by telling him to wait, by ignoring him or by acknowledging his presence with a comment like 'Did you', or 'That's nice', but then immediately returning to their chat with the first child. The following extracts illustrate these different fending techniques and demonstrate perhaps the most common adult ploys for sustaining chat over more than a couple or so turns.

Fending off

A: Can you tell me what you did at the weekend? 'Cause you had a lovely holiday, didn't you? (pause) Didn't you? (pause) Where did you go?
C: Torquay.
A: With your daddy?
c1: You know I just made . . .
A: Pardon? Yes, I'm watching. Did you go to the sea?
C: No, it was too cold.
A: So what did you do on the beach?

A: Oh! Who lives in Buckingham Palace?
C: The Queen.
A: The Queen. Yes. Have you ever seen the soldiers at Buckingham Palace?
c1: Mrs Russell . . . Mrs Russell . . .
C: No.
A: No? I went there once with my mummy and granny.
c1: Look!
A: And I saw the soldiers changing the guard. Do you

know the poem about changing the guard at Buck-
inham Palace?
c1: Mrs Russell . . . Mrs Russell . . .
c2: I do!
A: Can you tell me about it, Rachael?

There is clearly a genuine dilemma here for practitioners –
a real conflict between the desire to hold interesting and
sustained conversations on the one hand and the wish to
show interest in and concern for all the children present on
the other. By filtering various different offerings to accept
only those which fit the current focus of conversation,
teachers and playgroup workers ensure continuity of dialogue, but there is a danger that the whole course of
conversation may become adult dominated. The child's role
becomes that of a somewhat passive respondent. Notice in
the following transcripts how children, unlike adults, seldom
take 'double turns' in their move of a conversation. In other
words, if asked a question, for example, they usually answer
it but seldom go on to elaborate further. This means that if
the adult maintains the dialogue largely through questions,
children's answers tend to be terse and even monosyllabic.
Notice too that once the adult has the conversational bit
between her teeth, her questions may even override the
spontaneous offerings of the children. Indeed, the tendency
to ignore children, talk over them, and generally dominate
the proceedings, was the single most striking feature of the
recordings that our 24 practitioners responded to when they
read their own transcripts. Many were appalled and surprised by the blinkering effect that their own questions had
on their attention to what children were saying. The following are examples of what we called the 'programmatic' style
of conversation, the most dominant style found in our
recordings.

Nesting
A: Where do you think they build their nests?
C: They build them in trees.

A: Right at the very top of trees, don't they.

C: (breaks in) Yes they build them in . . .

A: (breaks in) Well that's a little sparrow.

C: Yeah, we . . .

A: (breaks in) I've got a story about a sparrow, that flew away from his mummy. His mummy told him not to fly too far because he was only a little baby one and he flew a long way and got tired and lost.

C: Well he . . .

A: (breaks in) He was naughty. Do you know what this little bird is?

C: Yeah.

A: What colour tummy has he got?

C: He's got the same colour as . . .

A: (breaks in) What colour is it? Do you know?

C: I've got . . .

A: (breaks in) I know it's the same colour as that. It's a beautiful colour. But what colour is it?

Holidays

A: You went to?

C: Chip fair.

A: Chipping? Oh, and what did you do on your holiday? Did you go to the seaside?

C: Yes.

A: Yes, and what did you do?

C: I played.

A: You played. Were there other children to play with you?

C: Yes.

A: What were their names?

C: I don't know.

A: You don't know. No? What sort of things did you play?

C: Different things.

A: What? Did you play in the sand?

C: Yes.

A: Ah. And did you buy ice creams? No? What did you do? Just play around in the sand?

C: Yes.

A: Was it nice coming home again?

C: Yes.

A: How did it feel to be home again?

C: Alright.

A: Alright. It's nice to come home when you've been away isn't it?

C: Yes.

A: Yes, back to your own bedroom, eh?

C: Yes.

A: Back to your own toys.

These two conversations are not the product of 'odd' adults. Sequences of question–answer–question–answer like these were quite common and they appeared in the majority of transcripts. They are so common in fact, that they may well indicate something quite basic about the task of getting young children active in conversation. Children, as we shall see in the next section, are very systematic in their response to adult questions – they usually answer them, seldom (about 7 per cent of the time) do they ignore them or change the subject. This means that a question from a (powerful) adult will almost always get the child talking. The problem is that he is unlikely to do any more than answer. Having taken his turn, he tends to shut up. Then it's the adult's turn again – another question will ensure another turn from the child, but little more. Thus adults characteristically get drawn into a continuous cycle of questions and answers.

But not always. Another style of adult conversation consisted of asking a question in order to get the child to say something, and then stepping back, taking the pressure off, either by making a response to the topic of conversation – a personal contribution – or by making an utterance which effectively filled their turn in the dialogue, but simply marked their presence and interest as a listener. Phrases like 'Did you?' 'Oh, how lovely' and so forth, following a child's answer to a question, signalled to him that he was being listened to, but left the way open for him to take another turn which was not driven by an adult question. These utterances we termed 'phatic' moves out of deference to Malinowski and Jackobsen, who first coined the term to cover similar aspects of language, used to maintain the 'atmosphere' of a conversation.

The wall

A: You don't know what her name is?
C: No.
A: Oh. She lives near does she?
C: Yeah.
A: Oh.
C: My daddy says don't climb up the wall because it hasn't been up cemented.
A: Oh, the wall's not very safe.
C: No, but I climb up but it's not . . .
(breaks in) Daddy doesn't like you climbing it.
C: No, because it might fall off.
A: Oh that would be dangerous wouldn't it, if it all fell, it all tumbled down with you on it?
C: Yes.
A: Mm. Sarah's gone to school today hasn't she?
C: Yes.
A: Did you go to her birthday party?
C: Yes. We had . . . different kinds of games.

The seaside

A: What did you do at the seaside?
C: I didn't catch any sun, 'cause we got no sun there.
A: (laughs) Did you swim?
C: No, it was too cold.
A: Was it? (sympathetically)
C: Nasty and cold.
A: Oh dear, that was a shame, wasn't it?
C: An 'an' we . . .

A: (interrupts) I thought you had said the other day that you had swum without your Daddy?

C: I did, that was in a swimming pool.

A: Oh . . . I see.

This style, by taking pressure off the child once he has responded to a question, enables him to elaborate on the theme and to take off in a direction that he chooses himself, presumably along the line that he feels is most interesting. However, the more prepared the adult is to follow through with a question after he has done this, the more likely it is that she will constrain the future course of their chat. In the two examples just considered, the main themes to be followed up and also the change in the course of a conversation were still managed largely through adult questions.

The transcripts just considered illustrate the tremendous difficulty that practitioners face in establishing and maintaining a style of dialogue which gets children involved in sustained conversations. In the course of our recordings, we did occasionally capture really complex episodes of conversation – always from adults involved with only one or two children. The following excerpts from these fail to do justice to the hard work being put in by the children – their tone of voice and the concentrated, determined sound of their talk clearly revealed the efforts they were making. But note how here too personal contributions from the adults continually lay bare their ideas and memories, giving the children a chance to respond to them. Note too how a practitioner sometimes 'adds up' what a child has been saying, puts in her own reactions and reflects these back to the child with a 'tag utterance' like 'Oh, you did, did you?'.

The bike

A: Oh, so it's quite a big bike.

C: Yes.

A: Ah.

c: And it's got, it's got um, it's got three um pedals and it's got the saddle, it's got the handbrakes, but it hasn't got the amb. lights; it wants the amb. thing, the amb.

a: The amber lights did you say?

c: It's got, it wants the amber lights.

a: Oh, it wants the amber lights. What are the amber lights for?

c: Well, they, they're for looking at, but you want some lights, don't you?

a: Well yes, just in case you ride in the dark.

c: Yes.

a: Then other people'll see you.

c: I must, I must, I must leave it at my Nanny Josie's because it's my only new bike.

a: And you must leave it there . . . what, so that you can use it when you visit your Nan? Oh, you are lucky aren't you.

c: But it's going to be painted red and black . . .

Puppies

a: The puppies have grown up and gone to new homes now?

c: No . . . not grown up . . . he might 'cause . . . he might be growing up. They're getting, they're getting heavy for me to hold but they're not, but they were always frightened of me.

a: The puppies were?

c: Hmm . . . sometimes.

a: I like puppies.

c: Hm . . . they're nice.

a: They jump up a lot, though, don't they?

c: Yes.

a: They jump on you when you're not expecting it.

c: Yes, but baby, but . . . kittens when . . . . cats don't do they?

a: Kittens don't . . . no they're not . . .

c: (interrupts) I used to hold aunty's one

A: Did you?

c: Hm . . .

The ogre

A: Do you know anyone that big?

c: Well once we . . . once we saw one, but he shouted at us.

A: You saw an ogre once?

c: No, not a real one, a pretend one. He kept shouting at us.

A: Where was that?

c: That was in . . . Banbury.

A: In Banbury there was a pretend one.

c: He kept shouting at us.

A: What did he (chuckles) shout at you?

c: I've forgotten now.

A: He had a big loud voice, did he?
Hm . . . and . . . and . . . he said I shall eat him . . .
Daddy said . . . our Daddy said . . . hm . . . he . . .
he . . . he . . . . oh, what him! Daddy said . . . .
Daddy just said, he said, and the giant . . . . I said
'would the giant eat us?', and Daddy said 'if you
make a noise it will'.

A: Do you think he would, love? (gently)

c: He might just bite us.

The control of conversations: a more formal analysis

We have already analysed adult talk with children from a number of perspectives – to see how far it was connected with for instance management or instruction, to see who initiated the interactions, and so on. But our purpose here is quite different. In the first pages of this chapter we have been discussing quite subtle differences in the structure of conversation and relying largely on the readers' intuitions as a basis for evaluating the differences we have described. In our discussions with teachers and playgroup workers during the active phases of the research we also relied on intuitions about what constitutes 'good' conversational style, although we tried to make sure that they were their intuitions and not ours. As we have already said, we endeavoured, where possible, to avoid making any value judgements ourselves; working from the premise that the practitioners were in the best position to decide how far what they read in the transcripts was consistent with their own goals. However, had we had the time, and had we thought up the following coding system early enough, we would have sharpened these intuitive judgements with a more formal analysis.

The problem with the presentation of transcripts such as those we have just read, is that it is easy to be very selective in picking them out and to ignore other episodes which present a quite different picture of what goes on in adult–child conversations. The deliberate or unconscious selection of data which happen to support one's preconceptions is clearly a danger. For this reason, any system for coding the conversations which handles all the data and gives an overall picture of what is going on is most desirable. But how do we achieve a coding system which reflects the sorts of interests we have been discussing?

The key to this problem, we found, lies in the notion of control. We ask 'How is the responsibility for controlling the course of conversation shared out between adults and children?' This turned out to be an extremely useful way of thinking about conversations since, as we shall see, it revealed differences which tied in neatly with our more global, intuitive judgements.

The 'control' of conversations

Imagine you are a third person, listening in to a chat between two others. Someone has just spoken and you are to ask yourself what predictions you can make about what the current listener is likely to say next. Try this out on the examples below.

Enforced repetition
1   Say 'bye bye' to Uncle Fred for me. (in play; child holding toy telephone)
Closed question
2   Are you going to Nanar's too? (her sister is)
Open question
3   Where are you going for your holidays?
Contribution
4   I liked going to the zoo when I was a little girl.
Phatic
5   Oh, lovely.

If we assume that the person listening to these different utterances honours their force and does not simply ignore or side step them, we can make a number of general predictions about what might follow next. In the first, of course, a compliant listener would say something about 'bye bye' to the imaginary Uncle Fred. This type of utterance has the force of an imperative, and specifies at least some of the actual wording in the ensuing utterance. We would not be at all surprised, as hypothetical third persons, if a child hearing this from teacher says to Uncle, 'Mrs Russell says bye bye', which did actually happen in one of our transcripts of a play sequence. The second utterance – a closed question – will probably lead to a 'yes' or 'no', then it could be followed, of course, by further elaborations on the topic. Here, then, one of two words – 'yes' or 'no' should figure in the preceding response. Number 3, open questions, specify the semantic category into which an acceptable next utterance should fall – in the example given, the child should talk about the 'where' of a forthcoming planned, or hoped-for holiday. Our uncertainty about what will be said next in the conversation has thus increased as the degree of control being exerted over the nature of the next step in the dialogue is gradually dropping. After a contribution like number 4, we are in even more doubt about what might follow. The person listening might well carry on with their own line of thought and not follow up such comments. It is not usually considered rude in a chat essentially to ignore these moves – as it would be, for example, to completely ignore the force of a question. Our listener might also comment on this utterance – 'Oh, I didn't know they had zoo's in those days', or ask a question 'Did you go very often?' They might also respond with a phatic utterance rather like that in number 5, 'Oh'. After a phatic utterance, we might well expect another comment from the listener or another move of the same type – 'Yes', a signal that the conversation or topic of conversation is drawing to a close, perhaps.

This simple scheme, then, offers a framework for looking at the control of conversations. The first three moves represent the attempted maintenance of control by the current speaker; contributions tacitly offer the locus of control to the listener who can, if he or she wishes, now take over the control by asking a question.

These are, of course, highly simplified options. Where, for example, the person listening to 1, 2 or 3 takes a double turn and, say, answers a question and then elaborates further, or asks one back, the course of future conversation can revert back into their hands. Furthermore, it is not always the case that questions must be responded to with an answer. For example, after example 2, the listener might ask 'When do you mean?' or 'Why do you want to know?' As we shall see, however, while this more complex set of options is exhibited by practitioners responding to children's utterances, they are not very often exhibited by children, who tend to honour the basic force of an utterance and then stop. They rarely follow questions by questions, for example, and seldom take double turns.

In the tables that follow, the distribution of these five basic types of move in adult and child turns in conversations are tabulated, together with the responses made by the listener. We see how many times, for example, practitioners ask children closed questions, and then we count up the number of times children respond simply with an answer or with some other type of response – like a double turn. Similarly, we look at the frequency with which children make spontaneous contributions and then see what follows them in practitioner talk. However, before looking at these tables, another aspect of the conversations needs to be described more fully – the 'tagging' of utterances.

A number of the adult's personal contributions ended with a question – 'There are lots of funny animals at the zoo, aren't there'. Similarly, with phatic utterances many tags were added, like, 'Oh, did you?' The incidence of such tag questions in adult talk was quite high (about 22 per cent of all conversational moves). Although they might seem rather like closed questions, demanding a 'yes' or 'no' response, we decided not to treat them as such because we judged that the aim of the adult was not really to ask such a question. We felt that the adults were not intending to call for an answer when tagging, so we decided to look at tag utterances separately, recognizing two main types – 'tag contributions' (4·2) and 'tag phatics' (5·2) like those just given.

In Table 4.1, we show the overall frequency of each type of move in adult conversation (drawn from second tapes where conversations were most frequent) together with the responses to those by the children involved. In Table 4.2, the mirror image pattern is presented, showing how adults ultimately follow children's different moves.

In these tables, the $\sqrt{}$ column refers to appropriate answers to a preceding question or tag utterance. The $\sqrt{4}$ column is where an answer to a question is immediately followed by a contribution (a double turn).

The most striking differences between these two tables is the much more systematic quality of the children's responses to adult talk. For example, after they have been asked an open question, 78 per cent of the time they produce an intelligible answer – rarely do they elaborate further on what they have said (5·4 per cent), almost never do they respond to such questions with one of their own. When an adult is asked such a question, however, her turn seldom consists

Adult's moves	Children's responses								
	2	3	4	5	√	√4	5·2	4·2	Other*
2	0	1	0	0	60	25	0	0	13
3	0	1	1	2	78	5	0	0	13
4	4	7	63	19	0	0	0	0	6
5	1	6	73	16	1	0	0	0	3
5·2	1	2	2	1	42	31	0	0	20
4·2	1	2	3	1	34	27	0	0	32

Table 4.1. *Children's responses to adult moves in conversation†* (only categories occupying more than 5 per cent of all adult moves are included)

* 'Other' responses include mainly those occasions on which the child being addressed, or another child, interrupts the conversation before the adult's move is responded to, or, as in phatics and contributions, where a response from the child was not necessarily called for and no verbal response was given.

† Where the adult takes more than one move in a turn in the conversation, her last move is used for this table.

Children's moves	Adults' responses									
	2	3	4	4·2	5	5·2	√	√4	1 + 5·1	Other
2	17	7	0	0	0	0	17	52	0	7
3	10	22	0	2	3	2	37	14	2	7
4	15	16	17	10	17	18	0	0	2	4
5	27	23	26	10	7	4	0	0	0	2
/	19	25	12	10	17	12	0	0	2	2
/4	22	19	9	15	16	16	0	0	1	1
Ignore/ interrupt	39	22	22	10	6	1	0	0	0	0

Table 4.2 *Adults' responses to children's moves in conversation*

simply of a direct answer alone (37 per cent). Indeed, adults are almost as likely to end their turn with a question of their own (32 per cent). Put another way – children are highly predictable in the part they play in a conversation – adults are not.

There are two different reasons why adults as a group are so unpredictable. In the first place, each of the 16 practitioners considered shows a wide range of responses to any given type of child move. For example, all of them sometimes answer the child's questions and then stop talking; all of them, on occasion at least, answer a question directly with another question. What this shows, as we might expect, is that adults have available a wide range of options in managing conversations. Children have far fewer. There are several reasons for the relatively stereotyped responses of children. Children of this age seem to find it difficult to think beyond their own response to anticipate where their answer will leave their listener. So it is unlikely that they are sophisticated enough mentally to indulge, say, in negotiating freely about the conditions under which they are prepared to answer a question. To make the point more clearly, consider the following (hypothetical) talk between two adults. Note how B only answers the question after he is sure that he knows what 'use' A is going to make of the answer. In short, adults often negotiate the context within which what they say will fall, to avoid any possible misunderstandings (though obviously we all fail at times!).

A: Are you going to come to town?
B: What time are you leaving?
A: Around six.
B: Is John going?
A: No.
B: Yes, I'll come with you.

There are, however, other possible reasons why children appear so stereotyped in their responses – why, for example, they do not often take double moves or ask questions in response to questions; reasons which have little to do with their dialogue skills *per se*. Our data illustrate clearly the power structure in adult–child conversations and this too plays a part.

	Questions	Contributions	Phatics	Replies	Other
Adults	40	20	17	17	6
Children	7	28	9	43	13

Table 4.3 *Composition of moves in adult and child speech* (expressed as percentages)*

* Where adult or child took a turn involving more than one move, only the last move was used for this table.

From Table 4.3, for example, we see that adults not only speak more, but a far higher proportion of their utterances are 'controlling' moves. Forty per cent of their 'final' moves in a turn are questions, compared with a figure of around 7 per cent of children's moves. Of the non-controlling moves, children score more highly, except in phatics. However child-centred adults are, then, the fact remains that they are adults – powerful beings who, while at the child's service, nonetheless provide the framework, constraints and rules within which he operates. Perhaps the paucity of questions and the lack of negotiation in child language reflect the social structure of the preschool as much or even more than it reflects the child's intellectual and linguistic abilities. To answer this question with any degree of confidence, we would need to look at conversations between child and parent or, even better, between child and child. One suspects that where the relationship is more genuinely egalitarian the range of inter-personal relationships and, hence, the making of cooperation, conflict and negotiation, will be dramatically increased. Unfortunately, we are not in a position to check out this possibility. Nonetheless, we can shed some light on the question by looking at the very marked differences in the way children respond to different adults, to which we now turn.

Conversational styles: getting children talking and questioning

We have already said that the greater variability in adult and child speech is partly a reflection of the fact that adults in general display a wider range of options in their conversational moves. But the greater variety is not simply a reflection of the adults' general sophistication in dialogue. The averages shown in Tables 4.1, 4.2 and 4.3 mask wide individual differences in adult style. An examination of these brings us back to the sorts of characteristics we examined more informally in the early transcripts in this chapter.

In discussing the earlier transcripts, we introduced the notion of programmatic talkers who, in conversation, display a number of characteristics. We might expect them, for example, to maintain the theme of conversation by continually asking directing questions; to pick up only those spontaneous contributions by children that fit in with their theme; and to ignore or fend off other offerings from children. In terms of our coding system, we would expect them to be high in open and closed questions, ignoring and those phatic moves that essentially serve to fend off children with competing ideas.

An excerpt from the recording that showed the highest incidence of adult control over the child's moves was given earlier – the 'Buckingham Palace' scene. That example was representative of this particular adult's recording in general – a high proportion of controlling conversational moves by her (76 per cent), a very low incidence of questions from the children (2 per cent); and also a relatively low incidence of contributions from children (22 per cent). However, this adult did not often ignore children, though she did frequently use phatics to fend them off.

The adult with the least controlling style on our particular measure asked relatively few questions and made a high proportion of contributions. Her tape was high in child questions and contributions and there was little ignoring or fending off of children. When we compare the children's language towards the two adults just discussed we find marked differences. Children talking with the second adult asked a significantly greater proportion of questions, (15 per cent against 2 per cent), made a higher proportion of contributions of their own (30 per cent against 22 per cent) and made a much greater number of double moves in which they not only answered a question, for example, but went on to elaborate on what was being talked about (21 per cent as opposed to 0 per cent). In short, then, the adult who exercised least control over children was much more likely to be questioned and to hear unsolicited ideas from children, and was far more likely to have her questions not simply answered but elaborated upon.

When we put together all the tapes on which conversation was taken as a major objective and subjected them to a statistical analysis (see Appendix C for details) we find that the pattern suggested by the comparison of the two adults above really does hold over the data as a whole. In sum, adults who offer children lots of their own personal views, ideas and observations receive the child's views back in return. Those who ask lots of questions tend to get answers but little more. The more an adult questions a child, the less likely he is to elaborate on his answers, to take double turns or to ask questions of his own. Too much control leads to children giving short, often monosyllabic answers and leaves them reluctant to take over control of the 'powerful' adult.

So far, we have talked as though the relationship between adult control and children's responses is entirely one way. It could be argued, of course, that adults only take control when they meet with a child who will not follow their contributions or keep going if they respond phatically. In other words, they only ask lots of questions when they are called for and hence are not responsible for the patterns found in children's moves. It may well be the case that some children are easy to get talking without questions while others are not. However, this cannot account for the bulk of our results. Generally speaking, all children followed contributions and phatics with contributions of their own. In other words, each of them responded conversationally to non-controlling adult moves, so adult questions are not the only device for keeping a child involved in dialogue. The programmatic style of much adult talk must, therefore, be more a product of the adult's personality or approach than of her children's capabilities.

The implication that follows from this conclusion is that it is within an adult's power to determine how conversations develop. Because children do respond so systematically an adult can maintain whatever style of conversation she wishes. By leaving the child more turns that are not directly controlled she provides an opportunity for him to put his own ideas into words and, on occasion at least, a chance to ask her questions. The apparent maturity and competence of the preschool child in conversation, then, is not only dependent upon his language ability, home background or whatever, but also upon the framework that the adult sets for him in dialogue. The more she is inclined or driven to ask questions and exercise control to keep him going, the less likely she is to be successful. By leaving the child time to think and, periodically, taking the pressure off to reveal something of her thoughts, she is most likely to see him at his linguistically most active.

There is, perhaps, little new in this recipe. Indeed, Isaacs (1936) drew much the same recommendations from her observations of children and adults at Maltinghouse. New or not new, however, it seems there are still lessons to be learned from these insights and a good deal we can do to encourage animated and interesting conversations with young children.

5

The language of the preschool

What do children aged from three to five years of age talk about with the adults who look after them in nursery schools and playgroups? Surprisingly, in spite of the large numbers of children now receiving preschool care and the importance of their language development for their general well being, the answer to this question is that we do not know. Although studies like those by Joan Tough (1977) and Barbara Tizard and her colleagues have shed some light onto the talk of preschool children, we have, as yet, relatively little to build on in our attempts to describe and evaluate the linguistic climate of preschool situations. In this chapter we look in some depth at the topics of conversation which figured most frequently in adult–child interactions on our recordings. As we shall see, the main findings discussed in this chapter are somewhat different in kind from those examined so far in the book.

In the study of the adult's roles in the preschool and our attempt to describe the different styles they bring to the fulfilment of these, we have been struck most by the tremendous variety of adult roles and styles. In the findings reported in this chapter, however, what is most striking is the marked degree of similarity in the nature and content of talk between adults and children. Indeed, we shall argue that talk in the preschool is constrained by a relatively clearly marked stage in the children's development. Furthermore, the preschool experience is timed and placed to offer the child an ideal launching pad for the next steps in his personal and linguistic growth. These experiences potentially complement home life and produce an interesting and important distance for the child between the experiences of family life and his new found life in the more public situation. In short, his preschool experiences cast the everyday content of his home life into relief, and provide the child with an abundant source of familiar yet potentially interesting and often amusing topics of conversation. We shall also find, however, that the incidence of really interesting talk is relatively rare. Most language addressed to the child is rather specific and related to the immediate context. However, where children initiate or are drawn into conversations about the past, striking events and happy memories, into speculations about the future and the exciting things that are in the offing, or when they talk about why events happen in the way that they do or why people are as they are – in fact, when talk is about more interesting and challenging things, the children do usually warm to the theme and maintain their part in the dialogue. In other words, it does not seem to be the case that children can only understand context bound talk. Our results suggest, in fact, that it is more likely to be the managerial, fast-moving nature of many contacts with adults that fosters mundane, context-dependent language.

In this chapter, we also explore in detail the topics and themes which figure frequently in the talk between adult and child. We also identify those topics of conversation which do get children going, using language in exciting and interesting ways. We also take some pains both in this chapter and Chapter 8 to try to identify some of the reasons why it is difficult for practitioners, with the best will in the world, to get involved with children in such exciting talk. In the preceding chapter, we suggested some features of young children's developing skills in conversation which make it hard to maintain sustained, egalitarian dialogues with them. In this one, we uncover fresh difficulties which tend to push adult and child in the direction of context specific language. We are not suggesting, then, that the task of the practitioner as a conversationalist is easy. We hope, however, that by thinking carefully about the things that seem to interest young children we might be able to make these problems a little less difficult.

Language away from home

Coming to our study of talk armed with few established indications from previous research in preschools as to what we would find there, our perceptions and expectations about what was going on were initially based on extrapolations from the relatively rich and recent studies of language between mother and child. Indeed, the psychologist's constant reference to 'motherese' – the somewhat ungainly title given to the way in which mothers adapt their talk to their children's level – caused some irritation amongst the practitioners working most closely with the researchers. They felt, rightly perhaps, that the description of language use between isolated mother–child pairs with infants and pre-preschoolers was of the most limited relevance and interest to people caring for groups of children in public situations. However, while the content of previous chapters demonstrate that they were basically justified in this reaction – it *is* different – there are some important insights to be gained from what we know about the course of early language acquisition to make predictions about what we might ideally find in the language of preschools.

When children first start to talk there is not enough content in their words alone to convey their meanings fully. In their first, single words, in the two-word stage and beyond, their speech is only comprehensible to a person in tune with their state of being – who knows where they are looking, what they are attending to, and observes their gestures, movements and so forth. From the first weeks of life, mother and infant begin the process of meshing their behaviour, ensuring that the mother often is in touch with what her baby is looking at, hooked on and potentially attending to (Scaife and Bruner, 1975; Schaffer, 1977). At the age of a year or so, when the infant enters and passes through the one- and two-word stages of language, his mental development is such that what he is thinking about is based in his present situation – in the here-and-now. Similarly, when mothers talk to such young children they too tend to talk about something tangible or salient among events around them (Snow and Ferguson, 1977). Thus, what is in the very young child's language is usually a clear reflection of that which fills his senses. Parents, when tuned into their child's activities and perceptions, are thus able to understand his impoverished speech and maintain conversations with him by exploiting his concentration on the immediate context.

As the child grows older, of course, the hold that the here-and-now exerts over his thinking and language becomes increasingly weak, as he develops his powers of memory, thinking and planning, and as he becomes more aware of his own likes and dislikes, wants and displeasures. As in the early stages of his language development, his parents' use of language reflects his level of development as, in their talk to him, they gradually extend the scope of what they talk about to refer to the past or the future, and to focus upon the needs and rights of people other than the child himself.

By the time the young preschooler is ready to enter the playgroup or nursery school, then, he is usually reasonably well equipped to talk to relative strangers not only about matters of immediate concern but also, as we saw in the last chapter, to talk about his experiences elsewhere, forthcoming events and the like. Generally speaking, the preschooler's grasp of grammar is sufficient to enable him to make himself intelligible to others, although his command of language and its structure is, of course, far from perfect. In the following very short transcripts we illustrate a few sources of grammatical difficulty for the child.

Pronoun potpourri
    c: Kerry is six.
    a:· Kerry's six. Who is Kerry?
    c: Kerry. He's a girl. She's my friend.

    a: You're going on three holidays – my goodness!
    c: And, and guess who we are going to see? Auntie Mattie – we haven't seen him for a long time.

Verbs – and auxiliary problems
  She was eaten too much.

It keeped fallin' in, keeped goin' fallin' in.

Self-evident as these grammatical difficulties are, they are seldom the focus of concern for adults. In fact, on our tapes they never were. The practitioners in their 12 hours or so of recordings never concerned themselves explicitly with teaching or correcting grammar, which is also typical of parental responses to young children's speech. Like parents, the adults' concern, when they gave their attention to a child, was on what he was trying to say rather than the manner in which he said it.

The children themselves appeared to be working hardest to communicate when they were trying to tell someone about a sequence of events and happenings that occurred in the past. Usually, the child had been the main actor in these little stories, but occasionally it was someone else centrally involved in some eye-catching or traumatic incident which had clearly left its mark on the child's memory. In these episodes – some were illustrated in the last chapter – the child was often grappling to get ideas into a correct logical, causal or temporal sequence; constantly paraphrasing and backtracking what he was trying to say. As he recalled one bit of explanation or description after another which needed to be inserted in his tale in order to explain properly how events had unfolded, he would often pause, start again, restate what he had said already and so on.

In the next two transcripts children are talking about sequences in which they themselves had not actually participated – they had been onlookers. In each case, getting the right words into the appropriate sequence stretched the children involved to their limits. Note the various 'errors' of grammar. These suggest that the children were using their language to the limits of their competence.

Easter eggs
  c: An' she had an easter egg and she did . . . (?)

A: And what was the easter egg made from?

C: Chocolate. An' she's been sick on it!

A: Poor Nicky, wasn't she very well? Or had she eaten too much?

C: She was eaten too much, an' she was being sick! (with considerable relish)

A: Oh dear . . . did that put you off eating your easter egg?

C: No.

A: No. (laughs)

C: When I eated it all . . . I didn't be sick.

A: I wonder why that was?

C: Because (stressed) – I don't be sick any day.

A: Oh good. You're strong and healthy are you?

C: Yes.

Stock car racing

C: The car turned over, and sparks came out . . . they found that they . . . (?)

A: Where did the sparks come from?

C: Um . . . out of the car.

A: Oh dear, so that car didn't win the race.

C: O' no, one, the yellow car . . . win . . . It catched up the . . . (?)

A: Did it?

C: And then . . . the red car . . . it won . . . two times.
(later)

C: We know, we know the number of the car, but I didn't know the number of the car what was the winner.

A: Oh, was there just one race or lots of races?

C: Lots of races. Some of them crashed . . . in the ditch, came sliding, crashed . . . you see?

C: And one of the cars that went along with no body left.

A: (laughs)

C: And no engine.

A: But he must have had an engine or he couldn't have gone along, could he?

C: Er . . . another car had to push him.

A: Oh, I see.

C: The winner car was pushing the one what not got an engine in.

In the next short transcripts, children are talking about their own past experiences or about things that might happen to them in the future. Again, the topic of conversation – accepted and developed if not initiated by the adult – largely pre-determines how sophisticated (and interesting) the dialogue will be. After talk about past and future comes an example of a rather didactic encounter in which the child's attention – controlled by the adult – is directed towards describing and naming rather mundane things.

The seaside

A: And what did you do, did you play on the beach and dig sand – big holes?

C: No, Daddy done some, but it was too wet, and it kept fallin' in but . . . not strong enough . . . kept fallin', kept goin' fallin' in 'cause it was wet.

A: Oh, I see.

C: We're going' on the big wheel (excitement in her voice) and we won't be . . . it keep birling (deliberate voice) and goes up and down. And when you stay up as well as somebody wants to go . . . uhmm . . . if somebody wants to get off, we . . . we would be at the top!

The farm

A: Have you seen pigs, Peter. Where did you see pigs?

C: In the pigsty.

A: Did you see cows when you went to the farm? Have you ever seen a cow?

C: No.

Apples
> A: Oh, that's a nice apple. What colour is it?
> C: Red.
> A: Do you like apples?
> C: Yes.
> A: Where do we get apples from?

The choice of topic, in company with the adult's style of conversation, basically determines the role played by the child. Some dialogues are relatively open and interesting – revealing genuine things that the adult could only find out from the child – a 'real' conversation. Others are basically closed. Listening in as an outsider, one is seldom in doubt how and in what direction the conversation is likely to develop.

In the next section, we see how typical these different types of interactions are and how the child's language changes as a consequence of the topic of conversation between adult and child.

Topics and domains of discourse

The task of analysing and classifying the content of talk between adults and children was relatively easy, though a little tedious. We simply looked at every utterance by the adult and determined who or what was being talked about and the temporal 'location' of what was being referred to – past, present, future, and so forth. The full list of categories appears below. We coded the adult's language rather than the child's for a number of reasons. The primary one was that we were only interested for this analysis in the topics which the adult participated in in conversation. Talk between children where it was overheard on the tape, and openings from children which were not taken up by the adult were not of interest here. By looking at the content of adult talk, we held up a mirror to that child talk in which she participated. We read through and analysed each of the initial documentary tapes twice – first identifying the temporal location in each utterance – what we called 'domain' of discourse – and then the topic of talk. Having classified every utterance by each adult in this way, we simply added up all the occurrences of each of the following categories:

Domain	Percentage of all utterances by adult
Here-and-now	69·7
Timeless	11·0
Long term past	9·5
Short-term future – planning	3·9
Long term future	3·0
Recent Past	2·8

Table 5.1 *Domains of discourse*

Some of these terms need a little explanation. The here-and-now is reasonably self-explanatory – talk about ongoing activity, what is currently being looked at, acted upon, and so forth. The timeless category includes a number of different aspects. Any enduring property of objects – their names, what they always or usually do; the reasons why people do or should do things; the logic of events, why some objects always do or must act in certain ways – all these are timeless properties of the human and physical worlds.

The long-term past refers to any happening or event which occurred before the particular playgroup or nursery school day, while a short-term past event is one which occurred earlier in that day – what Johnny did when he fell down; whether the child had had his milk earlier on and so forth. Similarly, the long-term future refers to something beyond the preschool day – forthcoming holidays; the photographer due tomorrow, and so on. The short-term future or planning language concerns what we will be doing later in the day after our present occupations – when are we going to have story time, who's coming to pick the child up at the end of the session and the like.

By an order of magnitude the most frequent domain of discourse was the here-and-now. But a sizeable minority of talk – just over 30 per cent – involved the language of past, future, logic, morality, or the properties of objects. One question of some interest was whether the pattern suggested by the figures in Table 5.1 was shared by all our practitioners. To answer this question, we employed a statistical technique for measuring the degree of similarity across adults in the frequency with which they used each category (see Appendix D). This revealed a substantial measure of agreement. The main reason for the agreement across recordings – which we discuss more fully later – was the common emphasis on the here and now. However, even when we left this category out of our calculations, there remained a low but significant degree of similarity of pattern, showing that the frequency of the less used categories also showed some agreement (Appendix D).

Our 24 practitioners then, despite being involved in very different activities and their very different styles of conversation and management, still showed a similar pattern of language use, in terms of the temporal character of what they talked about with their children. As we shall see, the same applies to the topics of conversation.

Topic	Percentage occurrence in adult talk
The child addressed	35·0
Objects and possessions	27·0
Imaginary people or things	7·1
Reason and logic	6·8
The adult herself	6·3
Absent people	5·3
Rules, practices and mores	5·3
Other present people	3·1
'We two'	1·8
'We the group'	1·5

Table 5.2 *Topics of discourse*

Talk about the child himself comes top of the list. About one in every three adult utterances was about something directly related to the child, his actions, perceptions and experiences. Next comes talk about things, followed, perhaps surprisingly, by talk about imaginary people in play, stories and make believe.

Reason and logic includes talk about mechanical causation – why wood floats; why water goes up a tube when we suck on it; why all the peas fell out of the tray when we sat on it, and so on. An adult rather infrequently talked with a child about herself, occasionally telling him what she was going to do – 'I'm just going to put Damon's apron on and then I'll come and talk to you', – and, much more rarely, about her own past experiences or future plans. Then comes talk about absent people – usually mum, dad, siblings and grandparents. Conflict situations, in which a child wants something which another already has, or which crop up when one child hits another, sometimes provoke the adult and child to discuss why people have to take turns, watch out for others, cooperate rather than fight and so on (rules, practices and mores).

Given the relatively large numbers of young children around, and the frequent arguments and clashes of interest overheard on the tapes, the 5·3 per cent figure for rules and practices is rather surprisingly low. It probably reflects the philosophy of many adults that, real danger apart, children should be left to sort out differences for themselves. In Chapter 2, recall, we reported what Janet had said, speaking to us over a tape as she watched her children, illustrating her intention not to get involved between children in their 'negotiations'.

Such reluctance to mediate between children also explains, perhaps, why there is so little mention of other children present in the room and so little group talk. The very infrequent incidence of talk about other people around illustrates another important point. Although playgroups and nursery schools work with groups of children, the major unit of interaction and talk is still the dyad – the adult–child pair. At least, when the adult is involved it is. It is interesting that in the data collected by Kathy Sylva and her colleagues, the child–child pair is also a prominent basis for the most extended and complex play and talk. These figures illustrate the very personal, one-to-one character of the contacts which young children have in the preschool situation. We discuss this more fully later.

When we examine the pattern of topics across all 24 practitioners on their documentary tapes we find, again, a good deal of agreement in terms of what is talked about most, less and least (Appendix D).

Talk about people and things

The detailed tables that we have just examined illustrate what we might well have expected, given the relatively high incidence of management and behaviour 'on the fly'. The most common subject for an utterance by a practitioner was the child she was addressing (35 per cent) and what she said only concerned his immediate activities or experiences (74 per cent of all mentions of the child).

Given the relatively high incidence of management demands in our initial recordings, together with those many fleeting contacts in which the adult simply commented on a child's activity *en passant*, this finding was perhaps to be expected. However, the most interesting aspects of our data on topics of dialogue are to be found in the remaining 75 per cent or so of adult–child contacts. To uncover these findings, we have to put our analysis of topics and domains together to ask the question 'Where is the person or thing being talked about located in time?' In answering this question, we gain some fresh insight into the way in which various aspects of the personal and physical world are introduced to the preschooler. As we shall see, for example, talk about people's habits, intentions, likes and dislikes take place in rather specific types of interaction between adult and child. Similarly talk about the past, present and future are concentrated in conversations about rather specific people and events.

This tabulation of our data shows in quite a graphic form those intersections of topics and domains that are relatively

References to the child involved in interaction (36 per cent of all topics)

A	B	C	D	E	F
Here-and-now	*Short-term-Future*	*Short-term Past*	*Long-term Future*	*Long-term Past*	*Timeless*
Management of action	Turns and requests	Culpability	Special events; 'Milestones'	Special events; traumas	Reasons for doing
Comments on action	Planning	Reasons			
Evaluations		Turns			
Suggestions					
Descriptions					

Percentage of talk about child in each domain:

A	B	C	D	E	F
74	5	3	4	10	4

References to objects and things (28 per cent of all topics)

A	B	C	D	E	F
Turns, requests	Turns	Turns	None	Presents	Descriptions
Instructions	Requests	Access			Properties
Play props					

Percentage of talk about objects in each domain:

A	B	C	D	E	F
70	1	1	0	10	18

References to 'imaginary others' (7 per cent of all topics)

A	B	C	D	E	F
Pretend to be/feel	Allocate role	Intentions	None	None	Reasons why
		Culpability			
		Describe what did			

Percentage of talk about imaginary others in each domain:

A	B	C	D	E	F
80	12	3	0	0	4

References to the logic of events (7 per cent of all topics)

A	B	C	D	E	F
'Why' happening	What will happen-prediction	Explain why happened	What going to happen	Remember what happened when	Always happens

Percentage of references to the logic of events in each domain

A	B	C	D	E	F
68	3	2	6	3	18

References to the adult herself (7 per cent of all topics)

A	B	C	D	E	F
Comment on own actions Assistance	Planning Promising	Following through	Special events	Special events – own childhood	Own character, make-up

Percentage of talk about adult herself in each domain:

A	B	C	D	E	F
83	6	2	1	3	4

References to absent others (5 per cent of all topics)

A	B	C	D	E	F
None	'Picking up' after preschool	Coming to preschool	Holidays Special events	Traumas Special events	Parents Habits and character

Percentage of talk about absent others in each domain:

A	B	C	D	E	F
0	1	2	10	30	57

Reasons why people do what they do (5 per cent of all topics)

A	B	C	D	E	F
What doing and why	What will do and why	What did and why	What will have to do when older and why	What did some time ago and why	'Always' do – mores

Percentage of talk about reasons in each domain:

A	B	C	D	E	F
81	2	2	1	3	11

References to other persons or people present in room (3 per cent of all topics)

A	B	C	D	E	F
What doing where	Turns Requests	Culpability Turns	Milestones Special events	Milestones Special events	Reasons why

Percentage of talk about present other in each domain:

A	B	C	D	E	F
78	7	8	2	3	2

Table 5.3 *Who is talked about, where and when and how often*

common (like the child's own past experiences, and the timeless properties of objects) and those which seldom or never occur. Instead of moving laboriously through the many different individual boxes in Table 5.3, however, we will draw out the major features of interest and discuss just these.

The current situation: 'you, me, present others and objects, we, and all of us'

Talk about people and things actually present in the room follows a similar pattern whether it is focused on the child, the adult, other children, the group, objects, or events currently taking place. The great majority of dialogue about these concerns the here-and-now (this accounts for 55 per cent of total talk). This talk arises largely out of management and the adults' comments upon what the children are doing. Concern with the short-term past and future does however differ a little from topic to topic. Only 2 per cent of the talk about objects concerns either their part in what has recently taken place or planning about the foreseeable future. At the other end of this particular scale, commentaries about other people in the room involve 15 per cent of this type of talk (but this is less than 1 per cent of the total talk). This feature of adult talk arises again largely through management and nurturance. When the victim of an attack comes hurt to the adult, she may well try to find out who did it in order to warn them against further excesses. Where there is an argument about access to materials or a request from the child to play in an already crowded activity, reference may be made to the activities of other children, often with a promise that in the near future the child can have his turn.

There are two other notable features of talk arising out of the current situation. References to the long-term past are relatively frequent in two categories – talk about the child's own past (3·5 per cent of the total) and the long-term past of objects (2·7 per cent of all talk). When we look in detail at the actual content of these conversations, we find quite a narrow range of things being talked about – and it is these that illustrate the timely relationship between the young child's stage of development and interest on the one hand and opportunities provided by the preschool experience on the other. Since these were of particular interest, we looked through all the transcripts of the documentary tapes and tabulated in some detail the themes that were being talked over. These are discussed in the next sections.

Holidays and outings

One very dominant theme in conversations about the child's past concerned special outings, holidays and visits. In all there were 169 individual references to these activities – holidays (54), special outings (54) to places like zoos (9), granny's or aunties, the seaside and beach (15). Arising out of such conversations were a number of references to diffe- rent animals (31) and the early beginnings of that great British pastime – moans about the weather. These have, however, a good way to go before reaching adult standards, coming in for only three mentions in talk about 54 holidays and 54 outings!

Traumatic events

There was a small but noticeable number of references to striking and serious events (21). Thirteen separate visits to hospital to mend broken bones or visit newborn siblings were mentioned. The local bobby came in for a couple of mentions as did firemen, GPs and others associated with dramatic life events.

Parties and birthdays

Getting old seems to be a major aspiration of preschoolers. Talk about age, size and important milestones crop up quite frequently with the young and conversations about parties, Christmas, birthdays, candles and games were also relatively frequent (35).

Home is where the memory is (much of the time)

Not surprisingly, by far the most likely theme to crop up in talk about the child's past concerned his home and family – mum, dad, siblings, the new car, stair carpet or bunk-bed, breakfast, tea and dinner, cornflakes and the milkman. Grandpas and nannies came in for a fair share of talk, as did toys at home, new possessions and the odd television pro- gramme. A total of 379 references were made to home and hearth (although many of these arose out of talk about absent others, rather than the child's own past experience *per se*).

The most striking thing about the preschool talk concern- ing the past and absent others is its domestic, banal quality. As Snow (1977) points out '. . . the most striking characteris- tic of mother's speech is its here-and-nowness, its everydayness . . . limited to what the child can see and hear, what he has just experienced or is just about to experience', (p.41). Here too adult and child are talking about everyday matters but now with minimal support from concrete events to help the child understand what is being discussed – the child has to imagine the people, events and happenings being discussed. Since the topics and themes are centred on him and his family, his general familiarity with what is being said no doubt helps him to make a start in the use of language in this highly representational way. Eventually, at best, he will be able to construct and play with rich imaginary pictures of the real and made-up worlds – here we see an early stage in this long-term process.

There are two notable features about conversations based in the past which we will return to at some length later. The first complements what we have just said about the home and hearth basis of much remembering. If one looks down the long-term-past column it is noticeable that when talk about absent others, self and objects (possessions) is removed, little else remains. There is very little talk about the adult's own past, for example. Because talk is usually centred on the child, it follows that he always has a rich source of personal experiences to help him in the conversation. Talk about the future and past of others, however, makes extra demands on him. He must use his general knowledge about things and people to play a full part in talk. A similar consideration arises out of the next feature of past talk.

Generally speaking, the past events that were talked about had the child himself as actor or joint actor. Visits, parties – all were events in which he had participated directly. Much more infrequent was talk about events in which he had only been a passive observer or where he had only been told about the event in question. 'Gossip' about something that so-and-so had told him was almost non-existent. If children of this age are ever involved in the development and perpetuation of rumours, it is not in the context of talk to practitioners. There were only a few occasions then in which the child talked about a series of events which he had only seen – we met some of these above. The retelling of such events in a coherent, logical sequence seemed to stretch children to their limits.

One final point about the character of talk about home and family needs to be made before we move on to consider the general question as to how one might set about the task of enriching conversations between practitioners and their children. This last point revolves around the finding that adult and child virtually never talk about the child's family in terms of what they are doing at the present time. Whereas talk about people who are present – the child included – is predominantly to do with their present experiences, as we have just seen – virtually none of the talk about absent others is. Is it perhaps the case that the young child is unwilling or unable to conceptualize what those near and dear to him are about while he lives on in playgroup? Do they continue to exist for him in a sort of temporal limbo, brought back when mum returns to pick him up from the group or school (the main basis for the 2 per cent short-term future references)? Until the child is able to talk clearly about those bits of his own life which he spends separated from his family it seems doubtful that he will be able to understand how life goes on for them when they are not with him. Certainly, we found none of our preschoolers wondering aloud what mum was doing now or what dad was up to. Whether such things are best left unsaid or are too difficult to think about we cannot say.

The majority of talk about mum, dad and others was, in fact, timeless. Children often talk about what 'mum always does', what she really likes, and always frowns upon. Timeless talk about the routines and regularities of home life, the attitudes, dispositions and feelings of members of the family formed a higher proportion of talk about others than similar talk on other topics, by an order of magnitude. Here too, then, the description of personal qualities, the way people do things and the effects they have on others, takes place in relation to those nearest, dearest and most familiar to the child. The practitioner is a natural audience for such talk. In playgroup or nursery school, mum can be an object of talk rather than a major participant in conversation, as she is at home.

The relatively high frequency of talk about absent others in past and future is a reflection of what was discussed earlier. This talk is mainly about holiday and special events, past or forthcoming, in which the family naturally plays a major role.

Are preschool conversations rich enough?

Almost 70 per cent of the talk between adult and child on the first documentary tapes concerned the here-and-now. About 7 per cent of remaining talk was largely managerial – concerned with the regulation of turns, timetabling of events and the like. At best, then, only one quarter of the time spent in talk was given over to considering the way people and things tick, to telling stories about events in the past or looking forward to things that might happen.

We really are not in a position to answer the question just raised above. We do not know what the talk between children of this age is like in any detail, for example, nor do we have any insights into the nature and content of talk between parents and their preschool-aged children. Mothers certainly have a much richer source of ideas about their children and their interests to build on in interesting conversations than practitioners do but it may well be the case that they have neither the time nor the interest to take part in such encounters. So the preschool experience might be either more or less interesting for the young child in this respect. As we have already pointed out, the timing of playgroup or nursery school life is well placed to extend the child's growing ability to talk about his home life and interesting past experiences, and may provide him with audiences which do not exist at home for such talk. Until we know more about the experiences and abilities of young children, however, we cannot say with any certainty whether or not enough is being made of the opportunities that exist for helping the child develop his language and imagination.

Having said this, however, it is notable that the major ingredient of much of the context-dependent language was its managerial nature – if the demands of responsive crisis management are reduced by better planning and worksharing, will the dialogues and other interactions between adults and children become richer and more interesting for both partners? This is one of the questions taken up in Chapter 8, where we examine the practitioners' desire and capacity to change their styles. It is also notable in this respect that many of the playgroup workers and teachers taking part did notice and regret quite frequent attempts from children to engage in conversations about events elsewhere that failed because they had not understood fully or listened attentively. All this suggests that there is considerably more potential in children for the joint exploration of ideas, memories and feelings with adults than is currently being exploited. We return to this question later, when we have looked in more detail at the nature of the adult's involvement in play and teaching.

6

'Teaching' the young child

Perhaps no subject is guaranteed to foster more arguments with preschool adults than that of their role as teacher. Although a contributor to *Contact*, the magazine of the Pre-School Playgroups Association, has suggested that the question of the preparation of preschool children for school should be considered by the playgroup movement, we suspect that many practitioners would strongly resist any attempt to cast them in the role of first teacher.

However, on their initial recordings, we found that approximately 20 per cent of all adult encounters with preschoolers were classified as instructional in nature. On the second tapes this rose to close on one third of all interactions. This result parallels Turner's (1977) findings which we discussed in Chapter 1. In part, this discrepancy between the practitioners' perception of their roles and what they actually do probably stems in part at least from the way we define instructional activity. However, we stick by the definition. It is perhaps fair to say that despite progressive education the everyday usage of the word teaching still conjures up images of text books, formal classroom layouts, exercises, and a curriculum given over to number, language and writing skills. However, recent research into adult–child interaction is stressing the vital importance of much more mundane interactions between children and their elders in laying the foundations for these achievements. When adult and child simply talk about things, play together or make things, they are preparing the basis for the child's eventual development of intelligent, directed learning. Instruction as we have defined it is consistent with this view of teaching and thus includes the adult's involvement in the child's practical activities at for instance the painting table, the woodwork bench, the wormery or the collage table. We have looked in some detail at the nature and quality of interactions in these practical activities. In line with current trends in research and education, we believe that these play an important role in developing not only the child's manual and physical abilities but also his powers of thought and language and his knowledge of others.

We have already acknowledged that conversation often hinges on subtle non-verbal cues – raised eyebrows, nods, smiles and postures – and these were inaccessible to us on our audio-recordings. Lack of access to what adult and child were doing while talking becomes an even more pressing problem when we try to understand and evaluate different styles of instruction, where so much rests on shared activity. Similarly, our lack of detailed knowledge about the children and their backgrounds also limits the scope and power of our analysis.

However, within these limitations, we gained enough insights from the recordings to see in instructional encounters similar basic styles of adult control to those already identified in conversation – programmatic, contingent and floating styles. And these, so far as we can tell, are associated with similar patterns of children's responses to those noted in Chapter 3.

In this chapter, we look at these various styles of instructing the young child and examine their relationships with children's activities. Our message is basically the same as that in Chapter 3. We will argue that the framework that the adult establishes by her style of working imposes marked constraints on what young children are set to learn from her. These observations lead us on, in turn, to suggest a number of general guidelines as to how one sets about the task of involving preschoolers in extended, interesting practical activities, and how one can help them to derive maximum benefit and pleasure from them.

Styles of instruction

In the following excerpt the adult maintains her involvement in the child's activity through control and questions. The questions this time are not primarily about absent people or past events as they tend to be in conversation, but refer to what is before the child's eyes.

Pictures in a book

A: What are they doing?
C: Catching fishes.
A: Catching fishes, that's right.
C: Hm.
A: What are they doing there?
C: Sandcastles.
A: Sandcastles, yes. Do you make sandcastles at the seaside?
C: I've forgotten how to make them now.
A: You've forgotten how to make them?
C: They keep falling down in . . .
A: Do they?
C: We went . . . we went . . . at . . . at . . . to the seaside.
A: Oh (pause) And what's that? What's that? What are they doing here?
C: I . . . I've been there.
A: What, what is it, look? That goes round and round, doesn't it? Do you know what is is called? (pause) It's called a roundabout. Have you been.
C: (interrupts) I don't know that roundabout.
A: Have you been on a roundabout?
  (later on).
A: Let's turn over the page then so that everyone can see. And there's another roundabout. That's in the park, isn't it?
C: Hm.
c1: What's that?
A: It's a roundabout. Have you been on one of these?

c1: Yes.

A: And did you like it? Where did you go on one?

c: Don't know, shopping.

A: Where did you go shopping?

c: Don't know.

Colours

A: And what colour's your dress Jeannie?

c: Blue.

A: Blue . . . have you got any blue, Stevie? Yes, your jumper's blue. What colour's your shoes?

Although we did find occurrences of such highly adult-controlled, instructional sequences, the programmatic style was far rarer in practical activity than it was in conversation. Because adult and child are, at best, sharing an experience, the problem of 'community knowledge', which often figures in conversational interactions, does not exist in instructional sequences. The task or activity creates a common basis of shared experiences for adult and child to build on. On some recordings, practitioners exploited the potential of task support to the full. Note in the following two transcripts how both adult and child are actively sharing the doing and experiencing of events. In the first, 'water play', there is an air of excitement and discovery – the sort of spontaneous discovery learning that educators like Isaacs and Froebel placed at the heart of their descriptions of effective early education. In the second episode, 'making puppets', the plan of action comes directly from the child. His mother has made puppets with him at home – but usually with paper. Here he elects to make a puppet from cardboard – but is not strong enough to cut it. So he uses the adult as a resource, an extension of his own intentions, and she, in turn, allows her actions to be controlled by him. However, in this last encounter, although the adult does follow the child and responds contingently to him, it is still she who makes the puppet. In the end, because it is she who has been active, it is not clear how far the child sees the product as his own.

Water play

A: Shall we listen to the water going down? (water noises)

JASMIN: That's where my water is going.

A: It is.

JASMIN: You can't see it.

A: Not yet, because you haven't put very much in it.

JASMIN: See it now?

A: I can see it yes, I can see it going down. There we are. There's the level of water. And it's getting higher and higher.

JASMIN: That's right.

A: Oh! What's happened? The tube's full so you can't get any more in. That one didn't take very long to fill, did it?

JASMIN: Put it higher.

A: Put it higher up? OK.

JASMIN: Can you see it? Let's have it. Whoops . . .

A: Laughs.

JASMIN: Up again.

A: What's happening now? (c and c1 speak at once.)

JASMIN: And guess what will happen?

A: Let's see what will happen then.

JASMIN: (Exclaims!)

A: You've fitted one you can't see through into the tube you can see through.

JASMIN: I'll do it . . .

A: Paul! Jasmin is just trying to see what's happening. You can't put that one right the way through because this tube's much smaller.

JASMIN: You know it's wrong size. Don't let the water go out. Put it the wrong way and then it won't keep falling out. OK?

A: OK Would you like me to hold it up, Jasmin?

JASMIN: (Exclamation!)

A: Can you see what's happening? Look! Jasmin, what's happening at this joint, there it's leaking out of there.

JASMIN: That's why it . . . Bit wobbly I am. (sound of water pouring fast) Stop!

A: Stop. It wasn't working quite as we wanted it to, was it? I wonder why? I think because there was a space between these two tubes.

JASMIN: I know, why don't we do it this way, mm?

A: We could try it that way, yes.
(sounds of water pouring)
It fits?

JASMIN: Stupid!

A: I don't think we can call a tube stupid. Can you? There we are. It does fit in the end that way.

JASMIN: (Exclaims!)

A: You'd still like me to hold it up?

JASMIN: Mm. (pouring sounds)

A: Oh. Pull.

JASMIN: Can you see?

A: Yes.

JASMIN: That's right. Oooops (water rushing)

A: (laughs) Pour it out from the spout.

JASMIN: Eh?

A: Look. See the water coming out of the spout over there? It comes a bit slower . . . see?

JASMIN: The water's coming out. What shall we do? What shall we do? (continues)

Making puppets

A: Richard. I thought you wanted to do something?

RICHARD: A puppet.

A: Well, what sort of puppet do you want to make?

RICHARD: Ummm. (pause) . . . Peeochio!

A: Pinocchio. Oh dear, and what do you think we need to make him with?

RICHARD: This.

A: Well come on, let's go over to the table where the scissors are then. Bring your paper.

RICHARD: No . . . I can't do it over there.

A: Can't do it where?

RICHARD: You can cut it, but you can't do these . . . the string to make it, to make it move. . . . Have to do it like a clown.

A: Yes, so what do you want? Do you want this (paper) or cardboard?

RICHARD: Card.
(later)

A: Is he a boy or is he a man?

RICHARD: He's a boy.

A: He's a boy, so he doesn't need to be too big?

RICHARD: No . . . That's it . . . put a cap on.

A: Oh well, I don't think I can . . . cut a cap shape, can I?

RICHARD: I can.

A: I think we'll just have his round head and make a cap afterwards.

RICHARD: No . . . he's got . . . a pointed . . . a pointed hat . . . at the top.

A: Yes, I see.

RICHARD: He has . . . a little ball on the top.

A: Oh well we could . . . what shall we make the ball out of then?

RICHARD: Put . . . one half there . . . I want that on.

A: Yes, all right then.

RICHARD: A little bauble.

A: A little bauble . . . Is that the right shape for his head?

RICHARD: Yes.
(later)

A: Right, that's his legs. Now what?

RICHARD: (very quickly) His arms.

A: His arms. Are they the same as his legs, or a
          different shape?
RICHARD: They've got fingers.
A: Oh, dear . . . (pause) . . . What sort of
          fingers?
RICHARD: One round one and some . . . all the rest are
          pointed.
A: I hope I can get the same number of fingers on
          this one Richard (smile in her voice).
RICHARD: Oh . . . one, two, three, one, two, three,
          four!
A: Yes, he's one short, isn't he? That's a shame.

After several more minutes hard work, however, Richard
decided to go off – before the puppet was finished. His span
of attention or interest seems to have been finally exhausted.

A: Oh there it is Richard.
RICHARD: Oh you can fix it.
A: Come back . . . come here a minute. What
          are you going to do now then?
RICHARD: . . . biscuits (gently).
A: Going to get your biscuits are you? All right
          then. Well you can finish it off after milk time.
RICHARD: Yes.
A: OK.
RICHARD: You can help me.

There are several interesting and important aspects of the
children's behaviour in these extensive episodes. (Each
occupied more than ten minutes of more or less continuous
contact.) In the first place, note how the children's language
is often concerned with what 'might', 'could' or 'should'
happen. They have moved away from literal, simple talk
about that which fills their senses, to trying to create
situations through their own or the adult's actions. To do this

they often take control of the adult's perceptions – 'Look', 'Watch that' – and of her actions – 'Hold this', 'Make a hole there', and so on. Such activities are at the very limit of young children's developing thought and language. They are beginning to move away from the dictatorship of the present, to help construct future states of the world. The fact that such episodes did occur shows not only that young children are sometimes capable of such complex achievements, but also that the preschool can accommodate them and that some practitioners at least have the ability to help the children bring their projects to fruition.

Before we consider the adult's part in these different episodes in detail, examine the next extract from a recording. The two we have just considered took place with relatively unstructured materials – water play and pieces of card and string. In both cases the plans originated largely in the minds of the children involved. Sylva and her colleagues found that many of the most extended and complex activities in the children they observed stemmed from work with structured materials, however – construction toys, jigsaws and the like. The next episode took place at the jigsaw table.

Making a jigsaw

	(noise of puzzle being tipped out)
SIMON:	. . . missing here?
A:	You'll have to start the right way up, you have to get them all turned over the right way.
STEPHANIE:	Can I do this?
A:	You can do that one, Stephanie, yes. I put that out for a little girl.
STEPHANIE:	I'm a big girl.
A:	Oh, you're a big girl. I'm sorry.
SIMON:	Does this go at the top?
A:	Yes, Simon. Look at the top of that clock again and that's the one that comes right at the very top. Look the big hand's on it. Can you see? Right, start off with that, alright?

SIMON:	This at the top.
A:	Now, that one comes next, doesn't it?
SIMON:	Then . . . then that one goes in there and that one goes in there!
A:	That's right. Now you've got the idea.
	(later)
A:	There's that one. That's it. Good boy.
SIMON:	That goes there?
A:	No.
SIMON:	That goes there.
A:	Good boy.
SIMON:	I'm doing very much.
A:	You're doing very much. That must be because you're four now, mustn't it?
SIMON:	Yes.
	(Following a conversation with another child some minutes later)
SIMON:	This one.
A:	It's not that one is it? Because that's . . .
SIMON:	Yeah!
A:	Clever boy. Clever old Mrs Russell because it's a hard one for me too. Good boy.
SIMON:	(inaudible)
A:	No, it's because you haven't got both backs . . . there you are then. Good.
SIMON:	That's it . . . where does that go, there?
A:	Look on the floor, there might be some pieces there.
	(later)
SIMON:	That's it.
A:	Good boy, Simon. Are you pleased about that?
SIMON:	Mmmm.
A:	That's a difficult one, isn't it?
SIMON:	Yes . . . it was a great big one.

This adult worked, on and off, for over seven minutes with this particular child – usually only coming in when asked for help. In between, she talked to and helped other children. It is unlikely that the child could have managed this jigsaw without her. At various junctures she reminded him to turn over pieces that he had forgotten to turn, told him to look on the floor for missing pieces and drew his attention to features of the puzzle that he should attend to in his search for relevant pieces. However, although she did occasionally help in the physical act of making the pieces fit, judging by the recording the child was quite capable of manipulating pieces, turning and fitting them himself, and she usually left him to do these tasks. It was 'his' jigsaw. She supplied the broader framework or scaffolding for him, filling the 'gaps' in the child's competence, and thus binding together his different, isolated acts of construction. At critical points, she made it possible for him to proceed where he would probably have failed on his own. He came, eventually, to complete what was, for him, a 'great big one'.

These sorts of interactions between adults and children are so common place in day-to-day life that it is easy to overlook their significance. We know from experimental studies that children are able to make things or do things with the help of an adult that they cannot yet manage alone. From the child's first halting steps, as he learns to walk, even earlier in his attempts to take possession of an object before he can reach skilfully, adults supply the framework within which what he can do can succeed. We also know from work with three- and four-year-olds, that where adults do not supply such a framework for the child in a difficult task, he may well become demoralized, losing interest in the activity and confidence in his own ability (e.g. Wood, Wood and Middleton, 1978). Yet, on our recordings, throwing the child back on his own resources was relatively common. Adults would often float by, offering the odd word of encouragement or isolated comments – but would not become enmeshed in extended interchanges. They thus essentially missed the opportunity for sustained encounters. The following illustrate some tactics for not getting involved with children.

Fending off

    c: I'm doing this hard one . . . look?
    a: So you are. Clever girl.
       (to a1 . . . Are you in tomorrow?)
    c: I can't do this one.
    a: Oh you can . . . you're a big boy now.
    c: Will you help me?
    a: Well, you just do it by yourself. I'm just going . . .
    c: Will you hold this for me?
    a: Well, I'll just hold that, but I've got to go and see to
       milk.

No doubt, some motivation for these ploys arose out of a need to fulfil other demands – the adults simply didn't have time. In part, however, they may have been inspired by the belief that children do best when left to their own devices – discovering things alone. While it is true that an overly programmatic approach by an adult does depress children's interest and involvement, it is unlikely that no help at all is the right prescription either. Sharing the activity with an adult is often a good stimulus to enjoyment, as Sylva and others have shown. Added to this is the fact that without an adult's overall framework the child simply will not succeed in many of the tasks he sets himself. If he is to leave a task feeling competent and successful, then, he will often need the support of someone more knowledgeable than himself.

In the jigsaw episode, unlike the water play session, the nature of the task itself made the child more reliant on the adult. Structured tasks – like jigsaws – have a right answer, and the access to this is through the adult. Though it may be more difficult to work with children in relatively unstructured task settings, these have the great advantage that they allow children more scope for setting goals and helping to achieve them. In both situations, however, the key feature of effective instruction lies in the adult's provision of an enabling framework – her actions must be contingent upon the child's efforts and interests.

What are the adults actually doing in these instructional

episodes? In the first place, as we have already said, they often supply the 'glue' that holds the whole enterprise together, helping the child to move on from one act or operation to the next, not allowing him to get swamped by too much complexity. They highlight things the child should attend to, drawing his attention to the effects of his actions, reminding him of constraints he should consider, and so on. They also help the child to maintain the right frame of mind for working things out. They stop him from becoming over-excited and hence losing hold of things; they sometimes reassure him that the task is a difficult one and that he is not silly or incompetent to be experiencing difficulty. They break the task down where necessary into manageable units so that he does not become submerged in difficulty. And they share and amplify his moments of triumph.

Many people have stressed the importance that these adult frameworkers hold out for the child. The adults involved are not simply showing him how to do the particular task in question, but also teaching him how to scrutinize and control his own learning and problem solving (Luria and Yudovich, 1972; Bruner, 1966; Wood, Bruner and Ross, 1976). The young child tends to be 'monopolized' by what lies immediately before his eyes. If he is to become a truly effective thinker and learner, he needs to be able to lift himself out of immediate happenings to weigh up possibilities, plan his actions and evaluate his efforts. This is precisely the sort of activity the skilled instructor is involved in. Where the child characteristically meets contingent, organized help he is provided not only with a chance to make a jigsaw, puppets or whatever, but with living models of intelligent self-control.

Another feature of these instructional encounters mirrors our analysis of conversations. This is the contingent adult's frequent use of personal contributions and sparing use of questions to keep things going. By expressing interest and a point of view, she helps emphasize the importance of what the child is experiencing. By reflecting back to him what he is currently doing or seeing, she helps cast his experiences into relief and to bring language itself alive by relating it to his immediate concerns. They also use physical events as turns in the interaction – letting actions themselves 'speak'. The things that the child can see, hear and feel, like conversational contributions, provide a potential springboard for his questions and commentaries. They carry the interaction forward, leaving the child with opportunities to take control and extend the enterprise. This, in turn, emphasizes the importance of the shared activity. Words and questions alone often leave the child cold. Although he may understand each word the adult says, words take on subtly different meanings in new situations. By relating her language and comments to the child's experiences the adult helps to bring these new meanings into being.

In the following excerpt we illustrate what may happen when the adult does not enmesh herself in the child's interests and activities, but relies on verbal interaction and questions alone to try and maintain his involvement. This transcript also illustrates another feature of instructional activity. It is taken from a recording made by the practitioner who was involved in water play with Jasmin. Here, however, the task she is involved in is a potentially dangerous one – cooking. Consequently, she has to keep far more control of the children's activities, so that they are not free to do what they please. She tries to keep the children involved by comments addressed to what she herself is doing or by questioning them about the material being used. The result, for some children at least, is loss of interest. The 'silly voice' starts to creep in, together with a few rather disruptive tactics from the children.

Baking

A: Shaun, you mix it now. You see it's getting a bit thicker.

C: I only get some.

A: Is the colour changing at all?

c1:   (breaks in) That is mine.

c2:   You can't have all of it.

A: Samantha (child starts sobbing). That's not going to go anywhere poppet. You're going to have a bit of this are you?

C: Is that flour?

A: No you taste it. If you just put the tip of your finger in and taste it.

C: Sugar.

A: What do you think it tastes like? Does it taste like flour?

C: No.

A: What do you think it is?

C: Sugar.

A: It is sugar, yes.
         (later)

A: Are you going to smell this? What does it smell like? Does it smell like anything you've had? Please stop eating it, Paul. What does it smell like?

C: Perfume.

A: Perfume? Where have you smelled that? Have you smelled that before?

C: No.

A: What does it smell like? Does it smell like your toothpaste at all?

C: Sugar.
         (Others echo 'Yes!')

A: Does it? It smells a little like toothpaste does it?

A: You shouldn't eat it not until later. When you get all your own piece you can.
         (later)

C: I'm going to eat my dinner.

A: (To A1) I'm sorry I couldn't get the matches.

C: I'm going to eat my dinner.

A: All right, Shaun! In the kitchen we don't run round do we?

SHAUN: No.

A: No. Why not?

C: . . . burnt. What's that?

A: Because you can get burnt. That's called a
      microphone. When the tape's finished we can
      all hear what we've been saying.

c1:   Da, da, da, da.

A: There's too much noise. That on the tape will
      sound like a lot of babies.

c: Da, da, da, da.

A1:   (in background) Don't push . . . if you slip
      you . . .

A: Just a lot of noise.

c: Da, da, da, da.

A: Some more please . . .

cs: Da, da, da, da.
      (children taking turns making noises)

A: Do you like all making the same noise or do you
      like to make a different noise?

c: Da, da, da, da.

A1:   Would you like to see how many children we've
      got, Shaun, this morning? Go and count them
      for me.

c: Da, da, da, da.

c1:   1, 2, 3, 4, 5, 6, 7, 8, 9, 10, 11.

A: Let's finish this off. There'll be some more
      washing up for us. (ignores continuing da, da,
      da's)

c: Da, da.

A2:   Is that good?

c: That's mine?

A2:   Are you cutting it?

c: But it . . .

c: No, cuppermint it.

A: It is peppermint, Sheena, that's right, we're
      making peppermint creams.

c: Da, da, da . . .

A: (da, da noises drown everything) You boys will
      have to go out of the kitchen if you're like that.
      It's dangerous with hot ovens.

The transcript to follow illustrates another feature of the adult's relationships with preschoolers – namely the tremendously 'inviting' quality in her actions. When young children see an adult doing things, they seem compelled to join in and do the same thing. Susan Isaacs commented on this same feature of young children's attitude to adults and used it quite self-consciously as a management device. She advised that where children were becoming boistrous or threatened each other's safety, the best tactic was not to admonish them or simply tell them to stop what they are doing, but to sit down and start working with some task or other. Once the adult was seated and working away, children would be drawn almost irresistably into her activities and peace would be restored. Where the adult can live up to the promise of her 'invitations' and handle the children who are drawn to her when she is doing things, then this tactic is an extremely effective way of involving children in activities. However, where a task is particularly dangerous it may well be a source of friction. Note, in the following session, how the adult, who is involved in mending a piece of playgroup equipment, is assailed with offers of help that she does not and, perhaps, cannot take up. The plan of action has to be her own and, in consequence, children are often fended off or ignored altogether. The lesson here, quite simply, is that the task itself helps dictate the adult's style. If dangerous or threatening activities are to be part of the preschool curriculum, then they must be bought at the cost of adult control. They are not well-suited to the abilities of young children who seldom seem content to simply look or listen to a commentary. They must act.

Mending the table

 A: We're going to mend the table, are we? We'd better bring it out then. Are you going to help me?

 C: Yes.

 A: We've got to mend the latch because its broken. I've got my hammer and look I've got the new latch. Can you hold the latch?

c: I know . . .

c1: (breaks in) I will . . .

a: You hold the latch, that's right. We don't need that because we've already got one of those. Who's going to bring the table out for me?

c: I am . . .

a: (breaks in) Lift it out. That's right. We'll do it just here at the bottom of the slide. There's nobody on the slide. Right. Well, what are you playing with then, David, because it should be on the table over there, shouldn't it? That's right. And the other piece. That's the lid. Where's the other piece?

c: Can I help you?

a: Right. This is the side piece that we're that's broken, isn't it? Now.

c: Can I help you?

a: (breaks in) We use the little nail. Can I just see the latch a moment.

c1: Can I help?

c: Can I help?

a: So let's put it down there. Yes, well you can watch because I think I'd better use the big hammer hadn't I? Oh, I've lost me nail. I had a nail. What did I do with it? Perhaps I put it in my . . .

Adult questions

In our analysis of both conversation and instruction we were struck by the tendency of some practitioners to ask children questions that they could clearly answer themselves. 'What colour are your new shoes?' 'What do coal lorries bring?' 'What's the name of that flower?' and so forth. Children often sounded rather reluctant to answer such questions, sometimes they said that they 'didn't know', and so forth.

It is reasonable to assume that at certain stages in the child's development these rather closed questions perform a valuable function. When mum looks at the picture book with her infant and says 'Oh, ... what's that?, she may be providing a valuable opportunity for him to practise and extend his vocabulary. But are such questions appropriate for rising-threes to rising-fives? They have a 'test-like' feel to them, in that the only basis for judging correctness is in the adult's head. But perhaps the preschooler, like the baby, does not recognize or appreciate this test-like quality. Maybe he is not aware enough of the state of other people's knowledge to appreciate that the adult already knows the answer to her own questions. If this is so, such questions may well seem legitimate and interesting to the child. Does the preschooler, then, realize when he is being asked to answer questions that the adult can already answer herself?

Our own data from the preschool recordings do not provide an answer to this question. We did find occurrences of children ignoring such adult questions, or refusing to acknowledge them. However, such refusals were simply not frequent enough to stand up to detailed statistical analysis. Consequently, we decided to undertake an independent study of children's awareness of other people's knowledge. This is not the place to review this study in any detail, but we will say enough about it to show how it does suggest that preschoolers are quite well aware of invalid questions.

We asked three groups of mothers to bring their four-year-olds into a playroom. One group of mothers played with their children and with a variety of attractive toys. Another group of mothers watched their children over closed circuit television as they played with another adult, using the same big box of toys. A third group simply sat and drank coffee, chatting to one of us while their children went off and played with the toys. The first two groups of mothers knew perfectly well what their children had been doing – but the children in the first group were also in a position to know that mother knew. The third group of mothers genuinely did not know.

After the children had played they went with mum into another room for a drink and biscuit and there the mother, at our request, tried to coax the child into talking about what he had been playing with, how he had played, what he had enjoyed and so forth. The results from the three groups were quite different. Generally, the children in the 'spy' group (where mother had watched them over closed-circuit television) coaxed their children into much more elaborate and sustained talk about what they had done. The group whose mothers had played with them were the least likely to talk freely, and mothers were often drawn into various devices like 'forgetting what happened' to coax their child to talk at all. It was quite clear that the children appreciated that mum could answer the questions herself and they often made their reluctance to play what was effectively a silly game quite plain. They sometimes told mum in no uncertain terms that she knew the answers to her own questions.

The group of mothers who knew nothing at all were also at a serious disadvantage. Children of this age need considerable support to recall past events, and if an adult is not able to offer intelligent 'guesses' (as the spy mums were) then the children often found the task of dredging their own memories and putting their thoughts into words too difficult or boring and readily gave up.

This result also illustrates the problems we noted in Chapter 4. Practitioners often do not know enough about the past events to which children are referring to provide a good framework to help them. This is one of the reasons, we feel, why they are sometimes found asking strings of questions to keep things going – including questions to which they already know the answer.

Effective instruction

Many practitioners may not feel that sustained instructional encounters with children in the preschool are a vital or even necessary part of their role. Against this, however, they should measure the possibility that young children – particularly those who come from homes where there is not the time or inclination to work 'projectfully' with the young child – often derive a good deal of potential benefit from such encounters. They are not only learning how to do a particular puzzle, or make a specific toy, but also being exposed to techniques of effective self-control which underly intelligent, directed and fulfilling activities.

For those who do accept this type of role, our observations here, in company with the results of other studies, yield a number of general practical guide-lines for effective teaching. Let us emphasize, however, as we did with conversation, that these are not prescriptions for adult-led activities. Work with young children has to be highly personal, revolving around their immediate interests or past experiences. We cannot supplement the intuitive, spontaneous sense of the adult as to what a particular child, in a specific place at a given time is likely to be interested in or prepared to work on. However, there are common plights in dealing with the young and some general rules of thumb which usually help in maintaining an interesting, 'egalitarian' relationship. The practical guidelines we offer below, will, we hope, be useful in the achievement of these. Many will appeal to common sense – against this, however, weigh the fact that they do not always or even typically govern the adult's style of working with the preschoolers.

- In trying to involve a child in an activity or maintain his interest in one already initiated, it is not usually enough to work through words alone. Adult actions invite the child far more strongly than her commentaries or questions. Once initiated, interactions fare better when the adult's commentary and questions relate to the actions that the child has initiated. These may be the child's own activities or those he has initiated from her.

- Where the child expresses difficulty or a need for help, do not continually throw him back on his own resources. A problem faced many times without success is demoralizing and breeds a sense of incompetence and failure.

• Against this advice, try not to set the child's task too low. Any operation which he is capable of or which he expresses a desire to try, should be left initially to him. By continually trying to 'step back' and by not following instruction with instruction or question with question, the child's level of ability may be fathomed. In other words, continually try to move back after giving help to see how things go, rather than jumping in immediately with further help.

• Let events speak for themselves. It is not usually effective to try and generate a sense of surprise, interest or questioning from the child by questions of one's own. Children's questions stem most readily from the adult's own responses to events or from events themselves.

• While children seem to enjoy 'adult' tasks, like baking and mending, these usually demand a great deal of adult control and are difficult to marry with a contingent approach to helping the children. Children like to act like adults, and will be reluctant simply to observe or participate through answering questions. If the aim is to foster joint activity, avoid dangerous tasks involving large numbers of children.

• Avoid questions to which you already know the answer and which you can be sure the child knows that you know. Talk about colours and shape occurs more naturally where they are an important ingredient in doing something – the colour of the next piece of the jigsaw or the shape of the next piece of Lego. By commenting 'over' the child's actions as he picks things up or works with them, the names and properties of things can be introduced to the child where he needs them and where they are relevant to his own plans and intentions.

• If the preschool group is to offer a wide range of tasks, some of which lie within children's competence and others which offer challenge and difficulty, the practitioners must be aware of the different roles that adults should ideally be prepared to fulfil. Easy tasks give a child the chance to practise self-control, help take pressure off him, and need not demand adult support. But where a child faces a challenge, and particularly where he asks for help, adult support can help him achieve his own objectives.

7

Adults at play

Most practitioners would probably accept that their role included management and conversation. Fewer would expect to play with their children, either from a conviction that this was not appropriate to children's development in the preschool or simply because they would feel uncomfortable doing so.

How much do adults play?

When we looked at opening remarks on the tapes, that is, at the initiation of interaction, we found that while everyone made openings in connection with management or conversation, they did not do so with play. Indeed, 12 out of 24 first tapes, just half, contained no opening remarks from an adult to do with play. The other tapes tended to contain only a small proportion of play initiations. But a few, which we will look at in more detail, contained a large one.

As we noted in Chapter 3, children's openings match the adult's. Thus, when the adults make few opening remarks to do with play, children also make few. The converse is true when an adult makes a large number of play openings. Children confirm the adult's expectation of her role. If she doesn't expect to play, children will not ask her to. She may be surprised to hear that there are preschools where the children *do* ask the adults to play. These, it seems, are the ones where the adults expect to, and so patterns of behaviour are set up. Viewed from within the preschool, there is no obvious reason for modifying them. But there is just a hint that adults may be more welcome as players than they think. Children, in fact, made slightly more play openings to adults than adults did to children.

A concentration on opening remarks alone, however, would clearly lead us to miss some play themes which developed out of openings concerning management, conversation or instruction. So we looked too at whole themes or episodes to do with play. These, as we saw in Chapter 3, represented about 6 per cent of all adult interactions with children. This gives us a better estimate of the extent of adult involvement in play, but it still has to be accepted that it seems generally rare.

Some of this apparent rarity may be an artefact of our recording methods. Play is often something done rather than something said. Looking at opening remarks or even whole exchanges may therefore underestimate it. Adults may often be playing alongside children, using the same materials such as dough or clay or sand, but not necessarily talking about what they are doing. It's a kind of parallel play. If there is talk it may be about something completely different from what they are doing or it may indeed be non-playful talk about the materials themselves. For example, while arranging blocks or cars with a child the adult may ask what roundabouts are for or whether he has ever seen a tractor like that one.

Why don't adults play more?

While we are aware that our recordings may not give the whole picture, the evidence from them suggests that most adults either do not see playing with children as part of their job, or at any rate see it as only a small part of that job. Incidentally, this is confirmed by Sylva's contemporary observational study of preschools in Oxfordshire, which showed little sign of adults playing with children or getting involved in their play themes (Sylva et al., 1980).

Why should this be so? Many practitioners see play as the child's business and not theirs. For example, one playgroup worker told us after making her first tapes that she believed it to be the job of the adult to provide a stimulus in the form of beautifully set out equipment and materials – good clean paint, fresh dough – and let the child get to work. She would not say to a child at the easel 'What have you painted?' or to another 'What are you doing?' because in so many areas an adult, by trying to talk to or play with children, only interrupts them. She would not join in imaginative play since an adult could upset a delicately balanced situation. It would be particularly wrong for the adult to intrude on something that was already happening. Others shared this view, fearing adult direction of play. Pretend play involving adults, they said, does not take the same course as play among children on their own. Adults spoil things. Janet, introduced in Chapter 2, felt that the kind of repetitive role that adults do tend to take on when they do get involved in play – accepting numerous 'cups of tea' for example – is not a profitable one.

These views are reflections of classical theories as to how children play and learn; of the Freudian view that a child learns to come to terms with his emotions and works through anxiety provoking events by means of play; of Piaget's view that play is a process of assimilation in which the child develops, fixes and retains new abilities, making sense of the world for himself; of the views of educationalists such as Froebel, Dewey, Gardner and de Lissa that in their play children are actively exploring the physical and social world; of Erikson's view that play strengthens the ego as the child masters his environment.

Many practitioners consider that adult intervention in play in the preschool should be kept to a minimum because the child himself is better able than the adult to select a direction of play which is most appropriate to his needs at the time. The adult is in danger of under- or over-estimating his ability, or of imposing on him her own ideas, which may inhibit or destroy his creativity. Another reason could be added. The preschool forms only part of the child's life. It may be more profitable for his time there to be spent in learning to play and share with other children, or to play and explore on his own – opportunities which may not be available at home in the same way. It must be emphasized that those who hold this view do not necessarily also deny a place to close adult–child relationships, including conversations and discussions in situations other than play. For example, one playgroup worker, Ruth, held long conversations with children in the book corner but did not normally choose to become involved in play.

A very real fear of practitioners' was that by joining in children's pretend play they might be making it more difficult for them to be clear about the difference between the real and the imaginary. At a stage when children may still be sorting out this difference, would it not be confusing to a child if an adult started pretending?

And there may have been another reason – pure embarrassment. The first clue to this arose during a meeting with playgroup workers and mothers at Deddington. They said that they did not play with the children at playgroup. One reluctantly admitted that she did enjoy playing with her own children at home. Others then agreed, describing how they too liked romping with their children, playing pretend games, and so on. Was it a surprise for each of these mothers to find that she was not the only childish soul who enjoyed letting her hair down with her children in private? It may well have been the case, because all agreed that in a public place they would not be seen playing with their children; they would not want to 'make fools of themselves'.

If playing in public is embarrassing, and in conflict with the 'respectable mother' role which many choose, it is not the only source of such role conflict. That occurs between the adult's roles within the preschool, too. It may perhaps be difficult for the playgroup supervisor or nursery teacher, responsible for the smooth running of the group, which includes managing adults as well as children, to forego this control in playing with children. To play with children means, as will become clearer soon, allowing them the possibility of controlling one. There may be a fear that the adult's authority overall, with both adults and with children, will be diminished if she lets this happen. And if this does not worry her, she may find it difficult to switch rapidly from one kind of role to another very different one.

Adults who play

We have looked at reasons why practitioners may not often play with children in the preschool. What happens when they do?

The tapes suggest that there are different ways of playing. We have labelled the adults with these different approaches as follows: parallel player, playmate or co-player, play tutor, and spokesman for reality. We will look at these in turn.

Parallel player

The adult may play parallel to a child using the same materials but without her play directly impinging on the child's play. For example:

> A: I like playing with this clay now I've started. It's not going to be very good! (Adult and child both laugh.)

The child may find the adult's presence comforting and supportive, even if there is no conversation, and he may spend longer at that activity than he would otherwise have done. Sylva's study found that children stay longer when an adult is around, even if they are not interacting. The child may also be influenced by the adult's play and he may find new interest in and ideas for using or combining materials. The value of the latter will be hotly debated since it is difficult to know where to draw the line between inspiring a child to try a new, sometimes difficult approach and inhibiting his exploration by providing him with a model to copy. A helpful rule of thumb is that you demonstrate new techniques for using materials rather than an end-product itself.

Playmate or co-player

The following game took place in a home corner (or was it dry sand?).

c: Do you have sugar? Do you have sugar?

A: Yes please, two spoonfuls, please.

c: Two spoonfuls. (with deliberation)

A: Have you any milk?

c: Yes, Hayley's going to give you some milk.

A: Jolly good.

c: You've got three.

A: Ah!! Gosh, that's sweet. It'll make me fat!

c: It don't matter.

A: Doesn't it? (to other c: Thank you)

c: No. I'll give some milk. There's for the milk, a bit more milk.

c1:   And I've got a lemon sweetener? There.

A: Yours is there. Thank you, lovely. Have I got to drink it now?

c1:   Yes.

A: All of it?

c1:   Yes. (laughs)

A: Mm, delicious. Just how I like it.

c: I gave you three spoonfuls.

A: That's right.

c: Would you like some more?

A: Yes please.

c: I'll have to get the teapot.

A: Have you boiled the kettle?

c: Yes. (pause)

c1:   I give you some tea.

A: Is that for me as well?

c1:   Yes.

A: Is that tea or coffee?

c1:   Yes . . .

A: Coffee? (child nods) Any sugar? (Child shakes head.) Oh, I can' drink it without sugar. (both laugh)

c1:   Sugar.

c: (at same time) I make you some.

A: Thank you.

c: I make you some with sugar.

A: Thank you.

C: I put sweet . . . in.

A: Oh you mean the Sweetex. That won't make me fat, will it?

C: Yes it will. I gave you eight spoonfuls.

A: Oh my goodness, it'll be like syrup! (all laugh) Ugh! Too sweet!

C: . . . give you some orange juice, with sugar in it.

A: Oh yes, that'd be nice. Orange juice with sugar?

C: Yes.

A: I think that's rather too many.

c1:   (counting slowly) One, two.

C: That's ever so sweet.

A: Well here we go then. Cheers!

c & c1: Cheers! (pretend drinking noises)

A: Mmm, wizard that was.

C: Your husband can have some.

A: Well he's not here is he? He's at work today.

C: I know but get a little boy to become to be your husband.

c2:   (asks for help.)

A: Yes, just a minute darling.

C: Get a little boy to pretend to be your husband.

A: A little boy. Well who's going to pretend to be?

c1:   No! (firmly)

A: Not you?

c1:   No.

A: Oh.

c1:   Mark will.

A: Will he?

C: Yes.

A: Why not you then Robert?

c1:   I don't want to.

A: Don't you?

C: A pretending one.

c1:   Hey, teacher, I've got some orange juice for you.

A: Thank you. Do you think we could have something else besides tea, coffee and orange juice in this cafe?

C: Yeah. We've got, plenty of beer, beer.

A: Oh dear, I don't like beer.

C: I have . . . cocoa (another child speaks at same time.)

A: Yes, cocoa would be fine.

C: Yes, and we've got drinking chocolate.

A: Drinking chocolate, yes. I'm not too keen on drinking chocolate. I'd rather have the cocoa.

C: . . . the chocolate, with cocoa, have to mix it up . . . sweeten it.

c1:   (breaks in) Two spoonfuls is all you want.

C: . . . of the mixture.

A: Yes.

C: Now you have to have eight spoonfuls.

The adult, Marion, is accepting a child's invitation to pretend. It is a very relaxed game with a lot of laughter. The adult is letting the children control the situation and, what's more, letting them control her. Let us look at the kind of questions she asks. Keeping the pretend theme, she asks for information, that is, she does not know the answers to her questions before she asks. For example, 'Have you any milk?' 'Is that tea or coffee?' 'Any sugar?' She also asks for instruction as to what she should do, for example, 'Have I got to drink it now? All of it?' Both kinds of questions give control of the content and actions in the game to the children. They also clarify what the game is about, for herself and perhaps also for the children. Otherwise she is mostly responding to them, thanking them for her tea and commenting on it. For example, 'Oh, I can't drink it without sugar'. Yet, as this last comment shows, without directing the game she is offering suggestions as to the direction that it might take. Again, for example, when a child says, 'I'll have to get the teapot', she asks, 'Have you boiled the kettle?' And later she says, 'Do you think we could have something else besides tea, coffee and orange juice in this café?'

There is little doubt, however, that the children are in command of what happens. For instance, when the adult says, 'The Sweetex, that won't make me fat will it?' the child gleefully replies, 'Yes it will, I gave you eight spoonfuls!'

The adult maintains the pretence all the time except for one moment when a child says, 'Your husband can have some' and she replies, 'Well he's not here is he? He's at work today.' Then the children become explicit that they are pretending, 'Get a little boy to pretend to be your husband', 'A pretending one'. There does not appear to be any confusion in their minds as to what is real and what is imagined.

There is a lot of humour and laughter in this play episode. All seem to be enjoying themselves in a very lively way. We have called the adult role that of 'playmate' or 'co-player' because she is playing side by side with the children and is deeply involved in their play. If the labels 'adult' and 'child' were removed from the transcript we might well lose sight of which was which.

Here is an excerpt from a tape made by the leader in the same preschool.

A: What are you making Andrew? (pause) What are you making Andrew?

C: Chips.

A: Chips. Oh, are we going to have some dinner then?

C: Not till morning time.

A: Oh, what are we going to do tonight then? Will we get hungry?

C: Yes. (both laugh)

A: Are chips your favourite?

C: Yes.

A: Chips aren't mine.

C: Look.

A: What are your favourite?

C: I like fish and bacon.

A: Fish and bacon? Together?
C: Yes.
A: Eerh! I don't think I'd like fish and bacon.
C: Oh it's nice. I like bacon.
A: With egg?
C: I don't like egg. My brother likes egg.
A: Your brother likes egg?
C: Yes, he eats them all up.
A: Does he?
C: Yes, and I say, stop looking at me.
A: Stop looking at you? What, when he's eating his egg?
C: Yes.

This begins as a pretend meal in which the adult has given the child control of the play theme, although her questioning role means that she is controlling the child's speech. It turns into a conversation about each others' likes and dislikes. There is mutual exchange of opinions, the adult as well as the child expressing how she feels. Although she doesn't continue as co-player she does address him as an equal.

Here she is on another occasion, joining in playing with Plasticine.

C: Aaaah!
A: Oh, here it comes again. Look after me. Oh I don't like that. Oh what is it?
C: My wriggly, my worm.
A: Oh what is it?
C: Look at my . . .
A: That's a big one. I'm going to make a bigger one than you.
c1: He's very . . .
C: Oh no you're not. (sing-song chanting)
A: Oh yes I a-am. (chanting too)
C: I'm making a longer one. (laughs)

And a little later.

> A: Oh come on, we've got to beat that Stephen. Look, his is longer than ours. Come on.
>
> C: . . . look how long yours is. (among a chorus of voices)
>
> A: Ugh! Take it away. Mine's longer than yours. (chanting) Ugh! Come on, hurry up.
>
> C: Mine's getting longer.
>
> A: Ooooh! (both laugh) You've got two now, it broke.
>
> C: And with that bit on was longer. (laughs)
>
> c1: Snakes.
>
> C: I'm going to stick it back together. (laughs) And mine is the biggest.

Without the labels, it would be very hard to distinguish adult from child. Control of action and of speech are entirely shared.

We wondered whether it were purely accidental that our impression of this preschool was one of exuberant talkative children. We wondered too whether the adults who are willing to be co-players with children are also those whose children join in most happily when it comes to adult-led group activities such as action songs and finger games. Perhaps their sense of playfulness communicates itself to the children; perhaps, too, these adults are more sensitive to what interests children and what they find boring.

Here is another example of an adult joining in a pretend game, again at the child's invitation.

Esther comes over to the painting easel where the adult, Rebecca, is talking to some children.

> ESTHER: Would you like to be my Grandma?
>
> A: Just a minute. Darren's telling me about his picture. I will be your Grandma in a minute.

Esther returns to the home corner and stays there alone. Rebecca follows in a minute or two after dealing with several other children (see the Preface). She goes to the Wendy house and knocks on the door.

A: Hello. I'm your Granny. I've come to visit you.
ESTHER: I've made you dinner.
A: Oh you have, thank you very much.
ESTHER: (breaks in) I'm just sitting down.
A: I'm very hungry. Now, there's some lovely dinner here. You've been very busy.
ESTHER: Yes, I baked it all. . . . I did manage. I've got all these babies.
A: You have got a lot of babies. Are the others all asleep?
ESTHER: Yes. 'Cept these.
A: Expect they'd like some dinner too, wouldn't they?
ESTHER: Yes.
A: Or have they had their dinner already?
ESTHER: No, that one hasn't. But those have. This one hasn't either.
A: Well, do we eat with our fingers or with knives and forks?
ESTHER: Yes, oh no. Here's an egg.
A: Oh, an egg. I'll take a sausage, I'll take a banana, and a . . . and a cup of tea.

Another new child, Jamie, comes into the Wendy house.

JAMIE: I'm going to be the Daddy now.
A: Oh you're going to be the Daddy, Jamie. Jamie, would you like to have some dinner with us? Perhaps you could pour us some coffee. I'll try to find my cup.
ESTHER: We need some more things on the table.
A: Oh perhaps we do need some more things on the table, yes.

In this excerpt the child, Esther, is quite at home with her chosen role of making dinner and coping with babies. She sets the theme and the adult follows it, for example, in saying, 'I'm very hungry, now there's some lovely dinner here'. The adult listens carefully to the child and asks questions extending the child's play theme. For example:

A: You have got a lot of babies. Are the others all asleep?

ESTHER: Yes. 'Cept these.

A: Expect they'd like some dinner too wouldn't they?

When Jamie comes in and says he's going to be Daddy, the adult, aware of the need to help a new child, quickly offers him a part in the game.

A: Jamie, would you like to have some dinner with us?

She offers him a specific job.

A: Perhaps you could pour us some coffee.

Esther observes.

ESTHER: We need some more things on the table.

And so appears to be accepting Jamie into the game. Esther goes on playing for some time; Jamie and the adult come and go meanwhile. Later on, the adult withdraws, leaving Esther and Jamie playing. She thanks them for her dinner and asks if she can return to finish it later. When later she does come back there is quite a party, with five children involved.

As with the previous games, the adult involved is pretending alongside the children, not directing the game but offering contributions which the children may or may not take up, and which may help to extend their thinking. The difference between Marion and Judy on the one hand and Rebecca on the other, lies mainly in their consciousness of what they were doing. The former were playing naturally and spontaneously. The latter was aware of what she hoped might happen as a result of her playing too.

Play tutor

In the conversation which follows the play theme is initiated by the children, but the direction the play takes is determined by the adult. It takes place at the Plasticine table.

A: What else do you need for your tea party?
c: Four cups.
A: Four cups.
c: Four cups. There's a lot of babies.
A: What shall we have to eat?
c: Dinner.

The adult then deals with another child who asked for help and then returns to the play theme.

A: A serviette. Do you have serviettes at your party? Yes? They're nice aren't they?
c: I've got some. I've got a cake.
A: You've got a cake?
c1: And I got a cake an' all too.
A: You're making a cake are you? How many candles are you going to have on your cake? (pause) You're making a cake just now, are you?
c: . . .
A: Here we are. (pause)
c: Now what next doing?
A: Well we've got the cups and saucers and cake. What else do we need?
c: Don't know.
A: What do you have at your birthday party?

c: A cup of tea.

A: A cup of tea? Do you have? . . .

c1: I have . . . at my party.

c: Make a kettle.

A: Make a kettle? Yes, we'll need a kettle to make the tea don't we.

c: Yes, got to do the tea.

A: Are you coming to join the party Michelle?

c: We need some pudding.

A: We need some pudding as well; yes we do, don't we?

c: Yes, and tea.

A: Who's coming to the party? (pause) Who shall we invite?

The adult is fully involved in the pretend theme. At first glance the situation looks like Esther's dinner party. However, here the adult is taking a much more dominant role. She is asking the children to think what they need for a birthday party. She follows up the children's suggestions when they are directly relevant to her theme, for example 'You've got a cake', and 'Yes we'll need a kettle'. She doesn't follow up the child's remark 'There's a lot of babies', but returns to her own with 'What shall we have to eat?' While it would be unwise to attach particular significance to a single instance, it often seems to be the case that the more the adult is directing a situation, play or otherwise, the less able she is to notice and follow up children's comments which are not central to her own thoughts. A familiar story, as we saw in Chapter 4.

In the next transcript the situation is less clear cut. The adult is pretending to have something wrong with her leg. The child is being the nurse.

c: On the patient?

A: I'm the patient . . . yes.

c: And . . . you . . .

A: Yes . . . better come and do something about it then.

C: ... and ... I'll ...

A: Come on then. (pause) ... There it is, there's the bad one. (pause) Where's the bandage? ... There's the bandage, just down here.

C: I can't find the bandages.

A: Yes, there is one. Lots of them down there.

C: ... Hm. Here's one ...

So far the adult is directing the action in the game, telling the child 'nurse' what to do. It continues:

C: ... Tied it up.

A: Oh, I think nurses have to do that, don't you? (pause) All right?

C: Yes.

A: Now, what do you have to do?

C: Tie it.

A: Mm ... and then what?

C: And ... and get you ... mm, a drink.

A: Oh, thank you very much.

C: There you are.

A: Oh lovely.

C: That's cocoa.

A: Lovely.

C: ... Here you are.

A: Thank you very much. I can eat it can I?

C: Yes.

A: Is that my lunch?

C: Yes.

A: Is that all I'm having for lunch?

C: That's, that's your dinner.

A: Oh, and what am I having for dinner.

C: Uhmm, fish.

A: Yes.

C: And, steak.

A: Steak!

C: Yes.

A: Oh! I love steak.

c: And peas.

a: Are you going to cook them for me?

c: Yes.

a: Lovely.

c: Now. (pause) There you are.

a: Thank you very much. Can I, can I have a knife and fork?

c: Yes. (pause) There you are.

a: Oh my leg hurts. Can I, can I have something to make the pain go away?

c: You can have your pills. (?)

a: Oh right, thank you.

c: . . . one. One for me. (?) That's all.

a: Thank you very much. What do I do with these then?

c: Eat them all up.

a: Eat them all . . . what with my dinner?

c: Yes.

a: Are you going to come and be doctor, Ian? I've got a bad leg.

c: I'm the nurse.

a: Right. I think you ought to come and have a look at my leg again, don't you?

c: Yes, I better . . . done up. It's not better yet.

a: Just a bit?

c: No.

a: Do you think you'll be able to do something with it?

c: Yes.

a: What?

c: Take the plaster off.

a: Ohhh   Well then what?

c: And . . . and it's not better yet. I better . . .

a: I've got a bad foot. (pause) (aside) The nurse has deserted me!

The adult is controlling both the child's actions and his speech at the beginning of this extract, by asking questions, for example, 'I think nurses have to do that don't you?', 'Now what do you have to do?', 'And then what?' Then the child finds what may be a more familiar role – providing food and drink – and takes over the direction of the action – providing cocoa, fish and steak! The adult then asks closed questions and so controls the child's speech. Her questions, however, are seeking permission or requests for information, for example, 'Can I have a knife and fork?' and these leave the child with control over the action. Dinner over, the child's contribution and control declines and he eventually goes away.

Spokesman for reality

We have seen the adult as playmate or co-player, sharing control of action and speech with the child. We have seen her as play tutor where she takes control. In both roles, she is entering into the spirit of the game, usually make-believe, and accepting a role in it for herself. At other times adults do not themselves undertake roles in the games but offer suggestions from outside. These suggestions may be intended to encourage a child to elaborate on or extend his play theme. Often, too, they draw the child's attention to what happens in reality and encourage him to make his game conform to the rules, physical and social, of the real world. We give an example of this below.

A:	What's that then, umm, Peter? (playing with cars and model village)
PETER:	A gate.
A:	That's a gate? Don't you think you ought to open it before you crash into it, mm? I mean you have to open a gate before you go through with a car, don't you?
PETER:	Mm.
A:	Else you'll damage the car.
AMANDA:	Else it will be broke down.
A:	It would be broke down.
AMANDA:	An' the policeman'll crash.

A: What would the policeman do?
AMANDA: Mend it.
A: He'd mend it would he? I don't think a policeman would mend the car. He'd take it to somebody that would mend it.
AMANDA: The shop.

In this game with cars and blocks, the adult, Joyce, is asking Peter and Amanda to reflect on 'what would happen if . . .?', that is, to think about the consequences of actions, both the logical consequences and the human reactions. For example, 'You have to open a gate before you go through with a car, don't you . . . Else you'll damage the car', points out the logical consequence of an action, while 'I don't think a policeman would mend the car. He'd take it to somebody that would mend it' is intended to be about what people would do as a result of the action.

Here is another part of the same conversation.

A: That's, that's a . . . what sort of house is that, Amanda?
AMANDA: A school.
A: A school house; so that's the school; so if you go in the drive it must take you to the school house, won't it. We've lots of rooms in there.
AMANDA: They're gonna bash it down!
A: Oh, I don't think so.
AMANDA: They're gonna bash it that way.
A: No . . . what would you do if somebody bashed into your house?
AMANDA: Have to go to the police, to Maureen's house.
A: Oh. Well, you'd have nowhere to sleep, would you, if they knocked your house down?
AMANDA: We could, sleep in . . . sleepin' bag.

A:	Well, where would you put the sleeping bag?
AMANDA:	On the floor.
A:	On the floor, but where, if your house is broken down?
CHRISTOPHER:	On the car.
A:	Oh, on, in the car, well . . .
AMANDA:	In the boot!
A:	In the boot, that wouldn't be very comfortable would it, if you slept in the boot?
CHRISTOPHER:	In, inside the car.
A:	Inside the car would be warmer wouldn't it?
CHRISTOPHER:	Mm.
AMANDA:	We have to have the wipers on (laughs, and A laughs too) If it's raining.
A:	If it's raining, yes.
AMANDA:	We have to have, we have to put the wellies in the boot. (laughs)
CHRISTOPHER:	. . . in the boot.
A:	You'd have to wrap up warm wouldn't you, if it was frosty, like today?

In the course of this discussion, the adult directs attention away from the original play theme towards a hypothetical situation. It is still an imaginary situation but no longer closely involved with the children's play. On other occasions the adult becomes an even stronger spokesman for reality. Probably unconsciously, she is constantly referring children to the real world rather than developing the play or transforming one game into another. In the extract which follows, the adult does not enter into a pretend game with a coal lorry but instead starts a discussion about how coal is delivered, what sort of fires one has at home and how they are lit.

A:	What's he doing then Christopher?
CHRISTOPHER:	He's a coal lorry.
A:	He's the coal lorry; what does the coal lorry do then?

CHRISTOPHER AND C TOGETHER:	Brings coal.
CHRISTOPHER:	They put sacks there, put sacks . . .
A:	In sacks?
CHRISTOPHER:	That's sacks to put it in.
A:	And what's in the sacks?
CHRISTOPHER:	Coal.
A:	Does your mummy have coal? Does she? Have you got a coal fire? to keep warm?
CHRISTOPHER:	Mmmm . . . they put it down(?)
AMANDA:	We got a fire in our house.
A:	You've got a coal fire, have you? Does Mummy have to light it? What does she light it with?
AMANDA:	(very quietly) Turn it on.
A:	She turns it on, does she? Oh well, you don't put paper and sticks on and then coal . . . to light it . . . no.
AMANDA:	No we have to do it this way.

Later on in the same game, we see the adult acting still as a spokesman for reality and using the game as a medium for instruction.

AMANDA:	And this must be a roundabout.
A:	That's a roundabout, yes. What do you do when you go to a roundabout?
AMANDA:	Swing on it.
CHRISTOPHER:	Go round it.
A:	Swing on it? Oh I, I think you do swing on a roundabout, yes.
AMANDA:	No, you swing on a swing.
A:	Oh, I see. Oh. (calls) Will you children come away from there!
CHRISTOPHER:	Oh, he's on the grass. Hi, look, he's on the path.
A:	Oh, he's on the, on the grass. . . . I don't think cars go on the grass, do they?

AMANDA:	We parked on it.
A:	You parked on the grass.
CHRISTOPHER:	Only wheels on the path, and, then they . . .
AMANDA:	(breaks in) We park in the drive, we park in the drive.
CHRISTOPHER:	. . . when we go somewhere.
A:	When you go somewhere?
AMANDA:	Daddy parks in his drive.
CHRISTOPHER:	We parks on the grass.
A:	He parks in his, in the drive, I think. I don't think you must park on the grass because the wheels, well what happens?
CHRISTOPHER:	Don't know.
A:	You get, very wet. And your tyres won't go round, will they? You get stuck.
AMANDA:	This one won't get stuck.
A:	What happens if you get stuck? Need to get a . . .
CHRISTOPHER:	New car.
A:	A new car! Oh, well I don't think you'd be able to afford a new car, would you? How about . . . mm?
AMANDA:	I got a new car . . . a white one.
A:	You'd have to go out and ring the garage up, wouldn't you?
AMANDA:	I got a white car.
A:	You've got a white car.
AMANDA:	Yes, and, a new one.
A:	A new one.
CHRISTOPHER:	An' we got a new car, it's red.
AMANDA:	We got a new car.
A:	What colour's yours?
AMANDA:	White and red.
A:	White and red. And your colours?
CHRISTOPHER:	Red.
A:	Red. Mine's white and blue. Is it a big car you've got or a little one?

CHRISTOPHER: Little one.
A: Like that one, mm?
CHRISTOPHER: Mmm.
AMANDA: Yeh.
CHRISTOPHER. . . . here another one. (car noises)
AMANDA: It's more like that.
CHRISTOPHER: It's a tree this is.
A: That's a tree.
CHRISTOPHER: Yes.
A: What sort of tree?
CHRISTOPHER: I don't know.
AMANDA: A tree stalk, a tree stalk.
CHRISTOPHER: (echoes) A tree stalk, a tree.
A: A tree stalk . . . oh . . .

As before, the adult is asking the children to predict what would happen and what people should do. For example, 'I don't think you must park on the grass because the wheels, well what happens?' and 'What happens if you get stuck? Need to get a . . .?' Later on, she asks questions about the nature of objects, for example, 'What colour's yours?', 'Is it a big car you've got or a little one?' 'What sort of tree?' The children's game does not appear to be disturbed by the adult's approach. They continue playing, and find inventive answers to her questions, for example 'It's a tree stalk'. However, they have little control over the conversation because the adult is asking lots of question to which they must respond.

This mixture of play and instruction occurs quite often on practitioners' tapes. Here is another example. In the following example the adult, Anne, at first spends considerable time involved in the pretend game of the children playing with dough. She shares control with the children, her remarks are personal contributions or rapport, 'I'm listening' comments. She uses questions very little. It is only later that she turns to instruction.

A: Did you put the cherry on the top of my cake?

c1: No. I thought, I'm going to make you a sandwich. I'm gonna make you . . .

c: (breaks in) Cream in it this time.

A: Oh, how delicious, I . . .

c: I'll make me one of with cream; 'cos I've I've sold out of jam.

A: You've sold out of jam, have you? So you're having to use cream instead, are you?

c: Yes.

A: Oh, I see.

c: Like ice-cream, ice-cream.

A: Oh, how lovely . . . Can I sit down? That's it. That's better.

c: I'm rolling it, making you a nice cake.

c1: I maked a bigger cake than you.

c: I'm making a roll with it.

c1: Shhhhhhhhhhhh!

A: What's that you're putting in now? Cream?

c1: (continues) Shh! (noise for putting in cream)

c: They've run out of jam.

A: They've run out of jam. My goodness, that's a big one. What's that?

c: Here you are.

c1: (shouts) A jam sausage, a jam sausage.

A: (at some time) I'd like a plate please.

c: Cherry!

A: I'd like it on a plate please. Oh, my goodness. Can I have a knife? I couldn't eat all that at once; I shall have to cut it . . .

c1: A cake, with a strawberry on the top.

A: Oh, thank you, a strawberry on the top.

c: Ha.

A: I do like strawberries, that's delicious, thank you.

c: And a raspberry.

A: And I like raspberries too.

At this point, the adult sees an opportunity for instruction. She starts teaching the child about halves and quarters. The exchange between adult and child changes gear. The adult starts asking questions, closed questions and ones to which she already knows the answers. The child gives brief, closed responses. Thus:

> A: Look, can I cut it in half? That's a half, isn't it, I've cut there?
>
> C: Yes.
>
> A: And then I cut it in half again. How many pieces have I cut now?
>
> C: Two.
>
> A: No. How many pieces have I got altogether? Now I've cut that one piece in half?
>
> c1: Ha ha! Look!
>
> C: One, two, three.
>
> A: Three, right. Shall I cut this piece in half as well?
>
> C: Yes.
>
> A: Now how many have I got?
>
> C: Four.
>
> c1: Then you'll have four.

The episode of instruction is quite short. The adult reverts to her play role. She pretends she has eaten too much and will get fat. The child, possibly confused by her change of role, reminds her that the game is pretend. The adult quickly asserts her recognition of the pretence before going on playing.

> C: This is a clean one.
>
> A: That's a clean one. I'll just have one of this. Would you like a piece of my jam sausage roll. Would you like a piece?
>
> C: Yes.
>
> c1: There's another little sausage roll.
>
> A: Oh, thank you. And another one. You're making that.

c1: And another one.

A: Oh, and another one, thank you. Oh, well I think I've eaten quite enough. I shall be getting fat now, won't I? Is that mine?

c1: It's pretend!

A: Well, I'm pretending I'll get fat, aren't I?

c1: . . . jam on top of toast. (c speaks at same time)

A: Well that's rather nice, isn't it, jam on top of toast.

Let us finish this section with another play situation, which the adult turns into instruction. The adult has been pretending to enjoy Sally's dough 'cake' and Sally has said she is going to make another one. She starts work on it.

A: You're going to make a pattern, are you, on the top. That's a good idea. (pause) Anyhow that's interesting, isn't it?

SALLY: Happy face.

A: It's a happy face, yes. What's missing on the face?

SALLY: Eyes. (pause) No, it's got the eyes.

A: Well, where's the eyes? It's got the eyes, hasn't it? And what else has it got?

SALLY: It's got, it hasn't got a nose.

A: It hasn't got a nose.

SALLY: It's got a . . .

A: (at same time) We could make a nose, couldn't we?

SALLY: Yes.

A: Yes. (pause) That's going to be a nice big nose.

SALLY: Not that big nose.

A: No, you want half that do you?

SALLY: That big.

A: Very good. Have a look at my face. Is there anything else on my face you could put on?

SALLY: A nose.

A: A nose, you've got a nose.

SALLY: Eyes.

A: Eyes.

SALLY: A mouth.

A: Yes.

SALLY: Teeth.

A: Teeth, yes.

SALLY: Hair. (pause) Hair.

A: Hair. Could you do something on your cake there to make some hair. You could, couldn't you?

SALLY: It's not big enough. I'll make another one.

A: No, I think that's rather nice. You could make . . . I think that's all right. By the time it's got hair on it'll look much bigger, won't it?

SALLY: That hair.

A: That's lovely, fine. What else. I've got something here which I don't think you can see unless I move my hair.

SALLY: Ears.

A: Yes. Have you got some ears?

SALLY: Yes.

A: Good. So how many ears do we need?

SALLY: Two.

A: That's lovely. Will they be as big as the nose, do you think?

SALLY: No, little ones.

A: Little ones. Look at my ears. Do you think they're bigger than my nose or . . .

SALLY: Yes.

A: Or smaller?

SALLY: Big.

A: Big. They're bigger than my nose, aren't they?

SALLY: Look!

A: That's fine, yes. Are they? That's lovely, yes, just right. You want another the same size unless your ears are different sizes are they?

SALLY: Yes.

A: They are. Are mine different sizes?

SALLY: (nods)

A: Do you think they are? Oh, I always thought they were the same size!

Should adults play with children in preschools?

One might say that children's basic needs in the preschool are for freedom from anxiety and from major bodily needs, for opportunity, for richness and challenge in the environment, for other children, and for encouragement from adults. Most practitioners try to provide these. Should they do more than provide and encourage? Should they ever get involved in children's play? In particular, should they get involved in pretend play?

We have mentioned that some practitioners have expressed serious doubts about the value of adults' playing. Adults may intrude, upset a delicately balanced situation and change the nature of the play. These are certainly valid grounds for concern, and adults may indeed have these effects. We have seen, however, some very different ways in which adults play with children, and that the effects on the children are also different.

A major concern about adult participation in pretend play in particular is that it will confuse children as to what was real and what was imaginary. Since we have some evidence from the tapes of practitioners who did play with children we can look at this problem more closely.

Remember this excerpt from Marion's tape where adult and children were pretending together.

A: That won't make me fat will it?
C: Yes it will, I gave you eight spoonfuls.

At one stage a child says: 'Your husband can have some'. Then the adult stops pretending and says: 'Well he's not here, is he? He's at work today', and it is the children who suggest that the pretend goes further: 'Get a little boy to pretend to be your husband'. The children are quite specific that it is pretend.

Anne finds herself in a similar situation eating pretend sausage rolls.

> A: Oh well I think I've eaten quite enough. I shall be getting fat now, won't I? Is that mine?
> C: It's pretend!
> A: Well, I'm pretending I'll get fat, aren't I?

Here it is the child who steps back and asserts that the game is only pretend, but the adult quickly reassures him that she knows that it is pretend too.

In the following excerpt Michael needs to continually reassert that his chocolates are pretend and that the adult should only pretend to take them.

> MICHAEL: Sweets.
> A: Oh, you've made some lovely chocolates with the clay, have you, Michael. Thank you. Mm, delicious.
> MICHAEL: Only pretend to take them.
> A: Mmm. Lovely, Michael.
> MICHAEL: Don't really take them, just pretend.
> A: (chuckles) Sticky chocolates aren't they?
> MICHAEL: Here you are (to other child) Don't really take them, Lizzy. Don't really.
> A: Everybody having chocolates.
> MICHAEL: Here you are, here you are. Do you want one?

Are Michael's reiterations that his chocolates are pretend necessary because the adult has not reassured him that she knows he is pretending? We cannot be sure. Yet it suggests why the adults in the following conversation were afterwards unhappy about what had happened.

> A1: What horse are you riding in the Derby then?

A: The winner.

MARY: (at same time) Sally . . .

A: Oh, Sally! Oh I don't think Sally's hardly in the
        class!

MARY: (at same time) Sally can race. She's she's a racing
        jump and she's a hunting jump.

A: Oh, she's a clever horse then.

A1:   Do you want your hat. Did you put your hat on,
        and your jodhpurs? How old are you?

MARY: Thirteen today.

A: Thirteen! You were only two yesterday.

MARY: I'm thirteen today.

A: You're thirteen today, are you? Oh.

A1:   Are you taking . . . with you?

Mary then breaks off to talk to a friend for a few moments
and then resumes:

MARY: Well I'm going off hunting tomorrow, and racing.

A: And who's going to take you?

MARY: (continues) We're winning. You'd love to see me
        winning.

A: Oh, we'd like to see you win. We'll have to come
        and watch.

MARY: No, you'll have to watch it on the telly.

A1:   Today?

MARY: No, tomorrow I'm going.

A1:   I'll watch it on the telly tomorrow then.
        Where's . . .

MARY: (breaks in) If I might be there.

A1:   Will you wave to me?

MARY: No, I can't do that because I'd fall off.

A: (laughs)

MARY: Fall off the blinking horse.

The child was deep in her fantasy and the two adults with her
were encouraging it, because it was delightful and amusing.
But was it satisfactory for the child? The adults were uneasy

about whether they should be letting the child fantasize at all. Yet the problem, we felt, was that the child needed help in drawing a line between what was real and what was imaginary but not so much in her own mind as in the adults. She needed to know that the adults knew when it was pretending. Only then, perhaps, could she safely enjoy her imaginary world.

We might conclude that the adult may join in pretend games without confusing children over what is real and what is imaginary so long as she is certain that the children know that they are pretending, and what's more, that they know that the adult too knows that the game is pretend. She may on occasion need to state this clearly before playing herself.

We will by no means be advocating that all practitioners should plunge willy-nilly into every play situation that they come across. We do suggest that the playing adult has something to contribute to children's play and to their development. The playing adult provides children with a model. This can affect children in three ways which Bandura and Walters (1963) have called disinhibitory, imitative and eliciting. First the child feels free to play. The playing adult awakens responses in the child, responses which may not necessarily match those of the adult. Secondly, the child may try to imitate the playing adult, in voice or action. Thirdly, the child is given ideas which stimulate him to think, to put together ideas previously unassociated, and to elaborate his thought and play.

Play for the young child consists of thinking in action. It is this thoughtfulness which is to be encouraged. And thought-fulness in both senses. A child needs to develop an ability for reasoned thought, for without it he cannot understand the world or establish his independence within it – he does not act, but only reacts. He needs, too, to develop thoughtful-ness about and for others, so that he can understand how other people are feeling and why they behave as they do, and develop feelings of concern and respect for others. Above all, he needs self-respect and this can only grow from his perception of others' respect and concern for him.

How can the playing adult foster a child's thoughtfulness and self-respect? We suggest a number of ways in which we think an adult may play with children in the preschool, taking into account the very real anxieties which have been expressed by practitioners.

Parallel play

An adult playing alongside but not with one or more children can provide a reassuring presence. She is indicating to the child that she is on the same level, metaphorically as well as literally, as he is. There is opportunity for conversation, about the materials or about something completely different. How the adult plays depends on her aim. For example, if her aim is reassurance she may choose to run the sand through her fingers or gently finger a lump of dough. If she plays above the level of the children she may give them new ideas on how to use or combine materials but it may be at the cost of depriving the child of making his own discoveries and of developing his own possibly unique approach. There is a genuine dilemma here. A child cannot possibly make for himself all the discoveries of a technological society, but unless he has an opportunity to experiment with materials and make discoveries for himself he may not readily develop the capacity for rational thought and problem-solving.

The adult as co-player

The adult co-player, as we have seen, shares or even hands over control of the situation to the child – control of both speech and action. The children's independence is maintained because they initiate and follow through the play theme. The adult only joins in an existing game and helps to sustain the theme by her comments and suggestions. This sort of play can be fun. The children learn that the adult is approachable and not a remote authority figure, and they may come to trust her more. They may also appreciate that adults have feelings too. The adult may learn to understand her children better. We had the impression that those adults who played with their children were also more sensitive to children's feelings when it came to adult-led group activities.

From her position on the fringe of the game, the adult may be able to draw in other children who would otherwise have difficulty in getting started. For example, Rebecca's finding Jamie a role in the game in the Wendy house. This subtle approach to getting a child involved can help children who find such situations a threatening 'sink or swim' affair, and who might otherwise take a long time to start playing with others.

Other occasions when an adult might choose to play are when the play is very repetitive or looks about to break down; or she may play with a child who does not normally concentrate on any activity for very long.

We hope that the adult player will try to be sensitive to the children, to leave the initiative with them, and to share control with them. She needs to be aware when she is intruding and when she is not. She knows that her suggestions will affect the nature of the game and so must decide when that is appropriate and when not. This is asking a lot of the adult and a rule of thumb might be helpful: Play with every child occasionally, play when you are invited to do so, and otherwise just watch. As you become more tuned-in to children through observing (see Sylva *et al.* (1980) on child-watching) your interventions will become more sensitive.

Play tutoring

To initiate play an adult must have a highly specific intention or else there is a risk of being heavy footed and spoiling everything. But initiating play may be helpful to children who do not readily play in the preschool or to children who do not play pretend games; for example, to the children of one practitioner who said pretend games were very rare in her group. Initiating play may be a way of helping other children with difficulties, perhaps in language development, in thinking logically, or in emotional development.

Smilansky (1968) called the play process 'pump priming'. If a child does not pretend she suggests that the adult play with the child and react as if the child were role playing. She might say, for example, 'How is your baby? Let's take her to the clinic. Here is Mrs Jones with her ill baby; can you help her please, nurse? Show the nurse where it hurts your baby.' She gives straightforward directions and establishes contact between the players. She offers suggestions, asks questions or explains behaviour. Here she stands outside the game herself, but she could also become a co-player, saying perhaps 'Let's pretend that . . .' An example Smilansky gives of encouraging a child to pretend, using objects similar to (but not miniatures of) real ones, has the adult saying, 'Let's say this is the room, these are the beds and this is the table. Daddy has gone to work and Mummy is cooking', or 'Mrs Smith, here's the medicine – it's pretend. Now call for a taxi; it's too cold for your baby to go out. Here's the telephone.'

A good way of initiating pretend play is to use a doll's house family. Marshall and Hahn (1967) described how they played, with one child at a time, with a doll's house and its family. To these they gradually added other people – grandparents, other families, a postman, a policeman, a doctor and nurse – and other places – a zoo, a farm, a doctor's surgery, a greengrocer's, a cafe, and so on (a list, note, remarkably like the 'favourite' themes of conversation reported in Chapter 5). They tried to introduce as many of the ideas as possible, finding that it was important for the adult to be stimulating (rather than warm!). Both Smilansky and Marshall found that childrens' subsequent dramatic play improved as a result of play tutoring.

Another play tutor, Joan Freyburg (1973) played with four children at a time, using pipe cleaner dolls and other materials to enact four prepared stories. She found that afterwards these children had improved in affect, imaginativeness and concentration, whilst a control group which had been given help with doing jigsaw puzzles and using construction toys, with equal warmth from the adult, remained unchanged.

Playing and thinking

These studies suggest that play tutoring, and role play in particular, can increase children's thoughtfulness in both senses, intellectual and social. If children play imaginative games they have to think symbolically, in the abstract, because they have to draw on their existing knowledge and experience and apply it to the theme they are enacting. If the game involves several children, the conflicting ideas of different players also provoke thought as the children become aware that others have different views from themselves which must somehow be reconciled if the game is to continue. It recalls to mind Brenda Crowe's famous story of two children from different social backgrounds playing in the home corner. The boy, stirring his saucepan, announced he was 'making stew'. The girl replied, 'You be the Daddy and make the stew and I'll just pop out to Fortnum's for the canapés'.

However, such challenging encounters in symbolic play were relatively rare in the observations of Sylva and her colleagues who found that 'pretend play' came well down on the list of challenging activities for preschoolers. Perhaps, then, the potential challenge of pretend is best realized when a sensitive adult is available to help.

Children who don't play pretend games and those who don't play with other children or those who only involve themselves in repetitive, role play, may be helped to play and to think by the playing adult, whether as co-player or play tutor. Other children may be helped to greater thoughtfulness by the adult as co-player. So too the adult who uses the play theme to refer to reality – if she is careful not to destroy the theme – provides the child with an exercise in hypothetical abstract thinking. For children's play to be respected by, and sometimes shared with, an adult, can only enhance children's self-respect.

8

Can adults change?

When our field-work with the 24 playgroup workers and nursery teachers was over, we sent them a brief questionnaire to ask for their reactions to their experiences in the research project. In particular, we invited them to tell us how, if at all, they felt that the experience had altered their views of themselves and their styles of working with young children. But we asked them first, whether in the light of subsequent events and the passage of some time, they felt that their original recordings still seemed representative of their initial style of work. The majority (17 out of the 19 who responded) said that it was. What they had recorded for us of their time in the preschool, portrayed in their own view, a fairly typical picture – warts and all. If that was indeed typical, could they in fact change any aspect of their ways of working? That is the question we try to answer in this chapter.

The first practitioners to make second, 'experimental' tapes were the two teachers and the playgroup supervisor introduced in Chapter 2 – Rebecca, Janet and Yvonne. Both Yvonne and Janet had been struck most in their documentary recordings by the high incidence of management in their dealings with children. Janet had been highly mobile during her recording and became involved in a good deal of directive management, while Yvonne had tried to engage a number of children in conversation only to find that the location she had selected – the milk table – continually pulled her into responsive management and the provision of services – which overrode her attempts to hold sustained interactions with individual children. Both went on, in their next recording, to try and fulfil the goal of getting to some 'depth' in their involvements with children. Janet sat down more, accompanied by different individual children, while Yvonne found a quiet spot to talk to one of her children about a fête which had recently taken place in their village.

Each of their subsequent recordings showed a dramatic drop in management, as they had planned, and the length and continuity of their interaction with children increased substantially. But their styles of conversation varied substantially as the following two transcripts illustrate. Janet talks about 'playing at home' and Yvonne about 'the fête'.

Playing at home

A: What are you going to do this weekend, Vicky? When you're at home.

VICKY: Um. Play with my toys.

C: Look! Look Mrs Russell!

A: (interrupts) What toys will you play with Vicky?

VICKY: Er, my teddy, my, me and my, erm, teddy.

C: Look, look I've done all the ... (A1 in background: Don't put the socks in your mouth).

VICKY: And, my erm ... (inaudible) And then ... my ...

C: Hey look!

VICKY: erm ...

C: Look Mrs Russell, I've put them together.

VICKY: All my toys I'm going to play with.

A: What sort of games will you play with your toys, Vicky?

VICKY: I haven't got any games.

A: No, but don't you play games with your toys? What do you make? Pretend things with them?

VICKY: Sometimes I ...

A: Yes, sometimes pretend things are called games.

VICKY: I play a cup and saucer game.

A: What's a cup and saucer game?

VICKY: Erm ...

A: You mean a tea set?

C: A tea set. I got one. I got, I got two saucers.

A: What do you do with your tea set?

VICKY: Pour water in it, pretend.

A: Pretend water – oh yes?

C: My mum sometimes let me have water in it.

A: Sometimes she really lets you have water. And then what do you do with it?

C: This . . . Mrs Russell . . .

VICKY: (in parallel) Drink it.

A: Do you play a game while you're doing that? A pretend game?

C: Mrs Russell . . .

VICKY: Yes. What do you play?

C: Mrs Russell. Mrs Russell it's for you.

VICKY: (inaudible)

A: Does she? And do you invite anybody to your tea parties when you have the water?

VICKY: No, because I've only got one cup and saucer.

A: Oh dear, then you can't have anybody in to tea, can you? (laughs)

C: I got two cups and saucers.

A: Do you invite, do you invite anybody to tea when you play with your tea cup and saucer?

C: My sister.

A: Oh yes, will you go and visit your Nanny this weekend Vicky?

VICKY: On Sundays.

A: Oh on Sundays. Do you always visit your Nanny on Sundays?

VICKY: Sometimes.

A: Only sometimes, not always. John what will you do when you get home from school today?

JOHN: Er, I will build, Buckingham Palace. (lots of background noise)

A: Pardon?

JOHN: Buckingham Palace.

A: What will you do?

JOHN: Buckingham Palace.

A: What about Buckingham Palace?

JOHN: Om . . . I'm going to do it.

A: What are you going to do with it?

JOHN: Build it.

A: Oh, you're going to build Buckingham Palace.

JOHN: Hm . . .

A: Ah, yes. And how will you build Buckingham Palace?

JOHN: With bricks.

A: Oh, do you mean Lego bricks?

JOHN: No.

A: No.

JOHN: Wooden bricks.

A: Wooden bricks, yes. Where do you build Buckingham Palace?

JOHN: Nowhere.

A: No? Where do you do it?

JOHN: I make it.

A: Where do you make it?

JOHN: Buckingham Palace.

A: No, listen. Where, where do you build Buckingham Palace? Do you build it in the kitchen?

JOHN: No, in the dining-room.

A: In the dining-room. Oh, do you do it on the table.

JOHN: Yes.

A: Hmmm. Doesn't your brother bother you when you're doing it?

JOHN: Hugh knock it, things down, Hugh knock things down.

A: Does Hugh knock Buckingham Palace down when you're doing it?

JOHN: Hm.

A: Yes, what do you do when he knocks the Buckingham Palace down?

JOHN: I build it all up again.

A: Oh! How discouraging. (sympathetic)

The fête

A: Ooh, on Saturday, I know what that was. That was the fête, wasn't it? Did you go?

C: I . . . I bought my clockwork car.

A: You bought a clockwork car, did you?

C: It's a racing car.

A: What . . . was there a toy stall?

C: Yes, and Mrs Edwards was there.

A: With Estelle?

C: Hmm . . . there was Ben Davis and . . . hm . . . . er . . . and Jonathan Roberts.

A: Jonathan Roberts. Hm . . . where do they live?

C: Hm . . . across the road . . . hm . . . hmmm . . . a bit near to our house.

A: Oh . . . in . . .

C: Across the road going like that . . . up like that.

A: I see.

C: See, our house is here and he goes up there.

A: Rather along . . .

C: He lives here.

A: Yes, I see . . . And were there many people at the fête on Saturday?

C: Lots and lots.

A: Were there?

C: Hm.

A: There will be lots of them camping there next week.

C: (interrupts) And they had . . . hm . . . they had an orchestra doing some mu -mu . . . doing some songs.

A: Did they? How lovely.

C: (interrupting) And you see they had a singing post and they had some wire on – on the bottom of the singing post . . . and had it to the orchestra. Whenever the music stopped on . . . on the or . . . orchestra . . . hm . . . they could ta . . . talk with the microp . . . for singing . . . hm . . . and then and then it comes out big . . . in big writing (?) up . . . . up in the orchestra.

A: Does it?

C: Hm . . . (inaudible)

A: It was a microphone?

C: Hm.

A: Was it . . . Yes? And . . .

C: (interrupts) They sing . . . with a micro . . . see they talk through the micro . . . phone. (hurray!)

A: They did, yes . . .

C: And all their talking went . . . through the wires and the orchestra the orchestra was, hm . . . doing some music . . . whenever it stopped you see, they could talk in the microphone all the way to the . . . orchestra.

A: It sound as if lots of things went on.

C: Hm.

(later)

C: And you see, then, you see they have a thing with tickets in and you pick out the ticket.

c1: (inaudible request – A: OK, you go and tell Mrs Harris.)

C: Whatever number it is . . . and you have to see what number, hm . . . it is on . . . hm . . . on the thing you use . . . and I won, I won a sponge bag . . .

A: Did you? All the items on the stall had a ticket on.

C: Hm . . . and the . . . and the same ticket.

A: (interrupts) . . . and the same ticket.

C: (in parallel) . . . one . . . was the object had on it the same ticket.

A: As you purchased.

C: Hmm . . . in the tin.

A: Yes, I see.

C: One's the same. One ticket . . .

A: (interrupts) But you paid.

C: (in parallel) . . . the same as another.

A: Have I got it right? You pay your tenpence and choose a ticket and then that same ticket is on the object on the stall?

c: And then . . . and then and . . . whatever prize . . . there's, that's the same as the ticket that you get out of the tin . . . you get!

a: Yes, Oh I see.

c: You win it. And he won it on that and I won a sponge bag on that.

a: You were lucky, James.

c: And I've got some shampoo in it . . . four-year-old's shampoo.

a: Oh I see. (laughing)

c: Some shampoo for four-year-olds. Yellow . . . it had a yellow four on it.

a: Did it?

c: On one of the sides . . .

In the excerpt from Janet's recording, note how her style of conversation is basically programmatic – she makes most of the running and only rarely does the child elaborate spontaneously on his answers to her questions or change the direction of the dialogue by asking questions of his own. Because Janet had not participated in the experience which the child had had and did not offer any personal contributions about her own involvement in any similar events, the child was not really given any basis for taking over control in carrying the conversation forward.

Yvonne's recording was quite different. Unlike Janet, she lived in a small village alongside most of her children, and the 'community knowledge' that she possessed – about shared events and happenings in the village – placed her in a perfect position to ask good leading questions and offer sensible and pertinent interpretations and observations of her own. She had not actually shared the child's experience of the fête, but knowing pretty well the sorts of thing that were likely to have gone on, who would have been there, and so forth, she had a wealth of background information to assist her in the task of being a good listener and contributor. Her transcript was quite high in personal contributions and phatic comments in which she continually reflected back to the child what he had said, often with an element of interpretation and extension. Whereas Janet, then, had little community knowledge to help the child along, Yvonne was well endowed with raw material for her part in the interaction.

Which would be more typical of our experimental recordings in general – an increase in adult questions in an attempt to keep talk going, or more contributions and a relaxed style? The increase in control of the dialogue on Janet's recording underlines the worry that she and many of the practitioners felt about deliberately setting out to engineer particular types of interaction with their young charges.

If the results reported in Chapter 4 generally hold true of conversations with preschoolers, then any overall increase in adult control will tend to systematically undermine the chance of getting children talking freely and animatedly. For by asking more questions the adult effectively creates a further barrier to the achievement of her objectives.

This same message came through on Rebecca's experimental tapes. Recall that on her first recording she had participated in children's play, talked with them about abstract concepts of time, number and shape, discussed past events and been caught up in an element of responsive management. Since she had already explored a whole range of activities, she went on, at our suggestion, to try and involve her children in even more challenging activities in which they might explore the logic of events in much greater depth. This Rebecca did, using illustrations to get children to make predictions about what characters in pictures might be about to do, why and to what effect. Her recording is illustrated next.

Picture arrangement
    A: You come and have a look. Roy, you've seen these before I expect, haven't you. Come and sit down by Gavin. Over there. Four pictures there, OK? Now shall I muddle them all up and you see if you can tell me which one happened first, when you look at

those? Have a good look at all of them. What's happening there?

c: Cutting.

a: Cutting. Cutting the cheese. So we'll put that one over there. Now what happens after you've cut it? What's happening in that picture?

c: Peeling off, that.

a: Peeling off the skin.

c: Hmm.

a: What do you have to do before you peel the skin off though, after that picture . . . she's holding it in her hand there, isn't she?

c: Hm.

a: She's holding it in her hand while she peels it, but in that one, she's still cutting it.

c: Hm.

a: And see how does she get it into her hand? Let's look at the other two pictures. What's she doing there?

c: Yes . . . touching.

a: Hm . . . And then she takes the . . .

c: (interrupts) Peels it.

a: Yes.

c: And then she

a: That's it, so can you put them in the right order? First the cutting and then taking the piece out, and then – just a minute . . . Do you think that's the right way round?

c: Hm.

a: That makes a funny, silly story.

c: Yeeeeees.

a: What happens in it?

On Rebecca's tape too, there was a marked (18 per cent) increase in the frequency of her questions compared with her first recording. In discussing the experimental tape at a subsequent meeting, Rebecca commented that she would not usually set out deliberately to get children involved in such difficult tasks – but would seize upon the opportunity if children themselves expressed an interest. It is clear that in this part of the recording her usual enabling style gives way to a much more programmatic approach. The task is the teacher's, not the child's. Indeed, it is interesting, in the episode that followed this one, how the child, wriggling like a worm on the hook, does her level best to change the subject away from the (for her) rather dreary chat about peeling skin off cheese, into much more fanciful chat about how it is possible – in somewhat distasteful circumstances – to be eating food after one has already eaten it. So much for sequential logic!

A: What's going on there. Laura, if you start with that one at the beginning?

C: She's peeling it first.

A: She's peeling it before she's even cut the piece out! And then what was she doing here?

C: She's peeling it and then, and then eating it again.

A: Eating it. I think she's, she's peeling it off, and then putting it back and cutting it, and then she's eating it, and then she's putting it back again.

C: Oh, ho ho.

A: Do you think, if you'd eaten that bit of cheese you could put it back in there again?

C: Noooooooo.

A: That's what happens when you eat something. Where does it go?

C: In your mouth. But if you didn't want it, you go sick.

A: Hm . . . yes. It could do. It could come out again, but it wouldn't because of the picture change would it?

C: No. It could come out, if when you sick though, if your tummy doesn't want it.

The same thing happens again later, with Gavin. He's asked to arrange pictures of a female person shown at different ages – baby, girl, mummy and grandma. He too seems to see little compulsion in the adult's view of possible realities.

Ageing

A: What would happen? First of all there's a granny. Then what happens?

C: There's a mummy.

A: And the granny becomes a mummy. Then what happens?

C: The mummy becomes a girl.

A: Hm . . .

C: Then the girl becomes a baby.

A: What happens to the baby? What would happen to the baby if you started off as grandma and you got younger and younger and became a mummy, and then you became younger and younger and became a girl, and then a tiny baby, what would happen to you after that?

C: You'd start growing again!

A: You'd come back and start growing all over again.

C: Yeeees. (silly voice)

A: That would be funny wouldn't it, if you got younger and younger and then older and older.

C: Hm.

The children's often ingenious rationalizations may make amusing reading – but do they, in fact, signal their reluctance to accept the task set by the adult? It is not possible from recordings such as ours to diagnose the possible significance of such wrigglings and contradictions, but the 'silly' voice adopted by the children, their often monosyllabic replies, and the readiness with which they accept a change in topic, all suggest that they are not finding these quite demanding tasks very enjoyable or comprehensible. Rebecca had to work hard to get the children involved and keep them going, and her language was far more prominent on these recordings than on her initial tape.

In her response to our questionnaire, Rebecca said that she had not really changed any of her style of working with children as a consequence of making the later tapes. This is hardly surprising, because we had effectively transformed the smooth running of a thoroughbred into the plodding steps of a workhorse. Rebecca's tape, then, not only illustrates the problem of engineering really effective teaching through a very didactic, controlling approach – it also underlines what we argued in Chapter 6. Effective teaching operates by confronting the child with dilemmas and problems – but ones that are not so difficult that they lie too far beyond his current level of understanding. We had pushed Rebecca into making more demands on her children – but we had pushed too far, too fast. In her spontaneous working with the children, she had adopted a more relaxed, responsive approach and this showed in the competence with which the children had responded to her. However, we should also note that on her first tape, she had involved her children in a great deal of more interesting and challenging activities than we found on many of the other documentary recordings. Arguably, then, she was already operating at the right level for her children – neither too far below their level of understanding, nor too far beyond it.

All three of our first collaborators displayed a great deal of flexibility in moving from their initial tapes to later ones. They showed extremely significant changes in their 'choice' of topics and domains and they cut down substantially on management. But in two out of the three cases, these changes had been bought at the cost of a good deal of adult control – would the same hold true of all our practitioners?

Out of context – into questions?

It is probably fair to say that the 24 practitioners were not particularly interested in our analysis of domains and topics, nor in our comments about the high incidence of talk about the here-and-now. They were struck much more forcibly by questions about who starts interactions, who keeps them going and how one ensures that a child is not ignored or fended off. As we have already said, many were cautious about and even opposed to the idea of deliberately trying to make things happen with children. The prevailing philosophy seems to be that the adult ideally waits for the child to show interest, offer a view or start a conversation rather than setting out to engineer these things. Thus a greater concern with listening to children and not fending them off, than with topics and domains in adult talk.

In view of this basic philosophy about the relationships between adult and child, we were quite prepared to find that while the incidence of management and fending off might well go down on the experimental tapes, there would be little or no change in the context dependency of language. We were half right. There was, in fact, a statistically significant shift in adult talk away from the here-and-now to an involvement in talk about the past, the future and about people who were not physically present – usually parents and siblings. While statistically significant, however, these changes were not particularly dramatic in practical terms. But looking at the overall change in this way is somewhat misleading. The experimental tapes made by different individuals showed various types of changes, and these were largely obscured by looking at the overall pattern.

Once again, it proved far more informative to look at individual patterns of working, in trying to draw a useful picture of what was going on.

From 'natural' to 'contrived' recordings

We began this analysis of individual 'styles' and changes in style by looking at the way that adults ended their 'turns' in interactions with their children on tapes 1 and 2. We asked whether they ended their turn with (a) a question, (b) a contribution of their own, (c) a phatic move, or (d) a response to a child's request or question. We then compared each practitioner's turn endings on tapes 1 to 2 to see if they had changed their style of responding to children. Was there any general pattern involved in the change-over from tapes 1 to 2? There was.

The tendency of teachers and playgroup workers to exert control over the interaction with their children by ending turns with a question increased significantly, by an average of 10 per cent (see Appendix D for details). This went hand in hand with reductions in rapport responses to children's overtures/questions and contributions. It seems, then, that any changes the practitioners had brought about in the nature of their interactions with children was brought at the cost of increased control. However, this general pattern masks some marked and interesting individual differences. Not all practitioners substantially increased their use of questions. Three out of the 16 who made second tapes asked fewer questions on their second tapes; they increased their own contributions and, in consequence, they met more questions and demands for response from children. Does this tell us anything about different adult styles of working with children? We think it does.

In reading through transcripts and comparing first and subsequent recordings we were struck by the fact that the adults who seemed to tell children a lot about themselves and their own views on tape 1 (i.e. made many personal contributions), seemed to maintain this style on tape 2. Consequently, we looked to see if those who revealed their own views and reactions to children most frequently on their documentary tapes did so on the experimental ones. By and large they did (see Appendix D for statistical details). We also wondered whether those who characteristically asked questions most frequently on the documentary tapes also did so on the second. They did not. Nor was there any pattern in the rapport and phatic moves.

From these observations, then, it seems that an adult's tendency to open up her own ideas before children is, so far as we can tell, a relatively stable personality characteristic – a facet of her regular working style with children. Questions and phatics seem to be more under situational or contextual control. They change significantly from tape to tape and adult to adult but they are apparently not a stable characteristic of an individual's working style.

What these conclusions suggest, quite simply, is that some adults are relatively good at holding sustained conversations and interactions with young children. More important, we suggest that they are good because they blend together their own views and ideas with their questions and phatic moves towards children. Rather than asking questions to keep things moving or to get the child thinking, or simply sitting back and making noises in the hope that the child will 'spontaneously' keep going, they often react to what the child says and does in a personal way. By doing this, they leave the child with an opportunity to run things – to take control of the interactions. They give him openings and some specific ideas to work with. If he wishes, he can treat their suggestions, comments, opinions and views as a basis for further thought and questions and not simply as demands that he has to meet.

This does not explain, however, why even some of the 'contingent' adults tended to increase their questions – although, as in Yvonne's case, only by a few per cent. The reason for this probably rests on the phasing out of fending off moves. In the following examples, drawn from the two tapes, we see how instead of simply making a noise when the child creates an opening, the adults involved show interest by following-up with a thematically related question.

From 'fending off' to 'conversation'

Tape 1
    c: I've finished my painting now.
    a: Lovely. You can paint now, Alison.

Tape 2: the same adult
    c: I've made a house.
    a: Super. Are you going to show mummy your house?
    c: Yes.
    a: You could put it in your bedroom at home.
    c: Yes, and I could play with it.

A: Do you have any little people to put in it?
C: I could put my play people in it.

The same shift away from isolated rapport moves, in order to take up an opportunity to initiate conversation is illustrated in the next two extracts.

Tape 1
    C: I'm going to my Nana's.
    A: You lucky girl.
    C: And I'm going away with my mummy and daddy.
    A: Super. Has everyone had their milk?

Tape 2: the same adult
    C: We've got a new T.V.
    A: Have you? Do you have any favourite programme?
    c1: I like Tarzan.
    C: An' I like playschool.

Questions used in this way – as genuine expressions of interest or as a prod to carry on talking about the theme introduced by the child seem to us, intuitively, to be enabling in nature. They help a child to carry through his intention to initiate an interaction with the adult (if, indeed, that's what he wants). It is those questions that follow on a number of rather reluctant offerings from the child, that cut across his conversational bows to change his topic of conversation, or demand information which he knows full well the adult already has, that seem to inhibit ready, interesting talk from young children. This is where personal contributions can fill an adult turn in an interesting and stimulating way – as we saw in Chapter 4. Once the child builds upon the adult's offering, perhaps by asking her a question or commenting on her turn, a genuine dialogue can be set up in which each partner carries some responsibility for the course taken.

Once again, then, in asking whether an increase in the adult's use of questions is a good thing, the answer seems to lie in the relationship between the question and the child's ongoing behaviour. Where it follows on a child's opening, it can act as an expression of interest in sharing talk. Where it extends the topic being explored into new and, for the child, interesting and understandable territory, as it is likely to do if it refers to events, happenings and people with whom he is familiar and knowledgeable, then it helps build a framework within which the child can remember, imagine and predict. But where questions follow one another in adult turn after adult turn – 'where', 'when', 'with whom', 'why', 'how' and so on, they signal that the child's interest is probably lost. He is unlikely to offer any 'new' ideas spontaneously, or to ask questions of his own. The rules of the game, once established, put him very much in the passenger seat, and he is unlikely to rise above the adult's control. And where he knows that the adult can answer her own questions perfectly well, like an adult he is likely to resent the fact – at least, he is unlikely to participate eagerly in the question–answer exchange. Test questions are a violation of normal conversational etiquette and the child seems intuitively aware of this fact.

Adults who showed only a small increase in questions on tape 2, but who maintained a high incidence of contributions, as Yvonne did, are usually, then, asking the extra questions to capture the children's attention and involvement. They are not being pulled into strings of questions by setting topics or activities which children are not interested in, nor are they continually asking questions which they can answer themselves. The minor increase in control exists simply to enable conversations to start.

However, where questions rise dramatically, say by over 15 per cent (as they did on five of the 16 recordings), the odds are that the adult's use of questions is becoming programmatic and overcontrolling. The two principal causes of such dramatic increases in questions are the selection of topics and tasks which are too far beyond the child's level of comprehension or which are alien to his interests, and the failure of the adult herself to give her own views and reactions – to expose something of herself for the child to work with.

Once again, then, we can only begin to judge the value of any type of adult activity with children – management, questions, play, instruction – if we know where and how the particular action fits in with the child's ongoing behaviour. Only an analysis which looks at the degree of contingency or meshing between adult turn and child turn helps us to decide whether a given type of move is likely to be productive or self-defeating. Consequently, we are not saying 'questions are out' any more than we argue that management is a 'bad thing'. It all depends on their context and their relationship to the child.

This analysis of patterns and styles of change from tapes 1 to 2 serve, then, to underline the points made in Chapter 4 which followed on the detailed examinations of the conversations that took place on tape 2. In view of the increase in control showed on these second recordings, it is probably the case that many of the most programmatic sequences illustrated in Chapter 4 were due, in part at least, to the fact that the adults concerned were deliberately trying to engineer particular types of interaction with children as requested. This leads us to doubt whether the style shown in our analyses are truly representative of any particular teacher and playgroup leader. However, whether this is the case or not, what the analysis of these joint experiments tell us about the children's responses to different styles of adult working still stands. The recordings may not be typical of the adult's general style of working, but the uniformity of children's response to adult moves is strong evidence that the relationships found between adult style and children's responses to these do have general significance.

Another aspect of the changes across tapes 1 and 2, recall, was the rather consistent nature of an adult's tendency to use, or not to use, personal contributions in talk with young children. As often happens, then, by attempting to change things – in this case adult styles of working – we also help to reveal that which is constant. What we need to do now is to see whether this finding will induce other adults to try and adopt this style of working with young children and whether, when they do so, they meet with some success. We return to this point in the final chapter.

Changes in topics and domains

We have already said that the language of the experimental tapes was less context bound than that on tapes 1. Practitioners tended to talk more about the past, and about timeless properties, and they changed the subjects they talked about. Overall, there was a drop of about 12 per cent in the frequency of talk about the here-and-now (Appendix D). The most marked changes across the two tapes was an increase in references to absent others and in references to the past. However, when we looked at the frequency of references to the child alone we found no overall change. (Statistically, there were 2 per cent fewer references to the child in adult talk on tapes 2, but this did not approach significance.)

These results reinforce the suggestion made in Chapter 4. They indicate a language of the preschool. In the first place, the tremendously high frequency of references to the child, coupled with the fact that there was no real shift away from such references when we move from tape 1 to 2, indicate that the child is, as it were, at the centre of the conversational universe. The temporal location of what is being talked about may change, references to people outside the room rather than to people and objects inside the room may increase, but the child's position remains unmoved. In other words, the practitioner's language revolves around him – his memories, perceptions and experiences. There is a pervasive tendency to keep language contingent upon the child's own perspective.

The major overall changes in reference to absent others and the past, usually took the form of talk about holidays, parents, new sisters or brothers, grandparents, the zoo – in fact, the topics of conversation already discussed in Chapter 5. The 'language' of the preschool, then, either revolves around the child's own immediate perception or it moves out of context to consider home and hearth, casting the child's own home life and family experiences into relief.

The one individual who most violated this tacit language of the preschool was Rebecca. She showed a very dramatic decrease in references to the child. Overall her tendency to talk about him dropped from 56 per cent of her utterances on tape 1 to only 14 per cent on tape 2. This was by far the most dramatic drop on the second tapes made. And this marked shift in teacher language away from the child's perspective went hand in hand with an 18 per cent increase in her questions.

We do not want to imply that the language addressed to the child must always centre on him and his experiences, however. We saw, in the chapters on conversation, play and instruction, that children themselves, given the opportunity, will sometimes ask questions about the adult and her background, take over control by telling her what to do, and so forth. Preschool children are not totally incapable of locking into the ideas and actions of others. However, any attempt to engineer a very dramatic change in the normal language and demands that are usually made of young children, seems to leave them cold, and leave the adult talking pretty much to herself. It was obvious, of course, that if we kept pushing practitioners into more and more demanding language, their relationships with the children would, at some point, start to break down. However, what we were most interested in was exactly where that breakdown occurred. Many of the practitioners who had initially been talking far more about the here-and-now than Rebecca did on her documentary tape, were able to lift the level of conversation on their second tape, moving away from labelling objects that were present or simply controlling the children's immediate activities, to talking about the child's experiences and things he had enjoyed elsewhere, or to talking about his family and what they were like. Their conversations did not necessarily break down – only when topics that were too far removed from home and hearth were raised, or where the adult became too programmatic, did the increase in demands on the child lead him to lose interest.

In general, our experience with the documentary tapes suggests that children have a far greater capacity for elaborate conversation, remembering, imagining and planning than they are usually asked to show in the preschool. If, then, one finds oneself continually in the job of asking children about the names and colours of things, or concerned entirely with what they should or should not be doing, the odds are that there are much more interesting and elaborate things one could be doing with them.

From conversation to play

Two of the practitioners who engaged children most frequently in conversation on tapes 1 and 2 – Ann and Ruth – went on, on their experimental tapes, to try and explore the imaginary domain by involving themselves in children's play. Both Ann, a teacher, and Ruth, a playgroup worker, had been extremely high in personal contributions and relatively low in questions on their initial tapes and their styles of conversation were both highly contingent. Indeed, several of the extracts used to illustrate contingent, non-programmatic styles of conversation in Chapter 4 were drawn from their opening tapes. They were natural conversationists.

Ruth, however, never involved herself in children's play. Ann was already a regular player and often joined in with children's pretend games. For Ruth, her experimental play tape took her for the very first time into the children's home corner. Ruth's style was transformed and not really for the better. She found that she was doing most of the talking in her attempts to get involved in play. The length of her exchanges with children plummeted in comparison with the long and elaborate conversations she had had in her conversations. Her personal contributions dropped by about 10 per cent (though she still remained the second highest in contributions on the second tapes – after Ann) and these were effectively replaced by an 11 per cent increase in her questions. She became more controlling, then, when she entered the play situation. One contributing factor, she felt, was that she was playing with the youngest children, but she also felt very ill at ease in the new activity and was less able to simply sit back and let the children take over. Here is an excerpt from her second tape – compare it with the episodes on her first tape ('The ogre' and 'Puppies'), on pages 70 and 71.

A: Are you going to put the nurse's cap on now? Do you see her going on? This nurse is going to look after us if we get sick, isn't she? Will you look after us, will you? What do you think, what do you think?

C: (breaks in) I want to wear this.

A: You want to wear that? Oh, you're going to be a nurse too, Fiona. Oh, I'm glad we've got a lot of nurses.

C: . . .

A: That makes me feel very safe because if I have an accident I shall have a nurse to look after me, won't I? Make me better.

c1: I want to be a nurse, I want to be a nurse.

A: You want to be a nurse too? Is there another one? Have a look and see if there's another one, Harriet. You might have to wait until one of these girls has finished.

c2: There isn't another one, I'm afraid there isn't another one.

A: No, when one of these, when either Fiona or Jane has finished being a nurse, then you can have a turn being a nurse, all right? Because I don't think there is another nurse's outfit. There we are. What about having a lovely evening dress, a special dinner dress, like mummy has. Would you like one or . . .? Hello, nurse Jane, have you got any patients today? Have you got any patients to look after?

JANE: Yes.

Ruth is doing all the work, trying to help children get involved in pretend roles once they have dressed up. She ends up doing most of the pretending herself. A great deal of management is involved too. Ruth was not happy about this and later wrote:

> I made my (experimental) tape in other areas of the play group where I do not normally intrude on the children (at Linnet's request). I found these were less natural places to chat and my tapes became dominated by my ideas and interrogations. I tend to feel it is better to leave the children to their own discoveries in many areas unless they invite one to join in.

In parts of the tape the children did invite her to join in. In these the children were involved in pretend roles and Ruth helped them to elaborate them. For example:

C: It's not burnt, it's not burnt yet.

A: Your dinner's not burnt? I'm glad it's not burnt.

C: Is that yours, is that yours?

A: Yes, that's mine. Put it back there to keep it safe. Thank you. What have you got in your saucepan?

C: This one's potato and this one's . . . peas. And this one's . . . I don't know what this one is.

A: You've got potatoes and peas and something else in there. You're not quite sure what that one is. Is that right? It smells nice. I think that smells a bit like gravy, do you? Mmm, smells lovely.

C: Smell this one.

A: In that one? That's the frying pan, isn't it?

c1: Look, Mummy, Mummy, Simon's dressed up as a cowboy.

A: Simon's a cowboy is he? Hello, cowboy Simon. What are you going to do today Simon cowboy?

c1: He's got the cowboy things on.

A: He has got the cowboy things on, hasn't he? That's a lovely badge. And lots of tackle. A picture of a cow down here.

c1:   . . . Cow

SIMON: I've been catching cows, catching cows.

A: You've been catching cows today? Were they difficult to catch?

SIMON: Not too difficult.

A: Not too difficult, that's good. You must be very good at catching them then.

SIMON: Yes, er I do. I used my lasso.

C: Are you going to sit down there?

A: You used your lasso, did you? You want me to sit down, Fiona? Yes all right. You used your lasso, did you?

c1:   (about dinner)

A: Your dinner's not ready yet.

C: When it's burnt you can have it, when it's burnt.

A: When it's burnt we can have it?

C: Yeah.

A: I don't like burnt dinner. I don't want my dinner burnt.

C: When it's hot.

A: When it's hot, oh, thank you; yes I'd like it hot, that would be very nice. You tell me when it's hot and I'll have some on my plate over there, all right?

C: Right.

Play continues for a few moments; then a child starts a new theme.

C: What do you think I am?

A: What are you?

C: What are you doing? I'm a . . . Will this give you a clue?

A: Will that give me a clue, um. Are you a fireman? Putting the fire out with your hose?

c: No.

a: Are you a policeman stopping the traffic?

c: No.

a: Oh dear, I wonder what you are.

c1: He's a, he's a . . . (noise)

c: It's in a, it's in a cartoon, but it isn't now. (two speak at once)

a: It's in a cartoon is it? And it's somebody who makes . . .

c: Spiderboy! (shouting indistinctly)

a: Um a . . .

c: Spiderboy! Spiderboy! Spiderboy! (shouting while adult speaks)

a: Sort of swishing noise, and holds their hands out, um. Oh that's difficult. I don't know.

c: It's Spiderman!

a: Oh, you're a Spiderman, I see

In the Spiderman exchange the children sounded very excited, perhaps because they were delighted at being in total control of the situation, the adult being unable to guess whom they are pretending to be.

Although Ruth did feel so ill at ease on her first attempt at play with the children, the relatively high frequency of personal contributions in her interactions, like 'Your dinner's not ready yet', 'I don't like burnt dinner. I don't want my dinner burnt', 'Oh, that's difficult. I don't know', all provide opportunities for children to take control back – which they did eventually start to do.

After making her experimental tapes, Ruth said that she now spent more time talking to and playing with children in different activities. She had decided to add player to her repertoire of roles. She had found pitfalls in adopting the new role, and remained cautious of dominating the children's activities by asking too many questions and making too many controlling suggestions. However, she felt that if children seemed to enjoy her being there and they showed signs of shaping her role in play, there were rewards to be gained –

particularly for the isolated child who had yet to find his place in play with other children.

Ann, already experienced in playing with her children, showed a much less dramatic change of style on her experimental recordings. Her questions actually went down by 10 per cent on her second tapes while her contributions increased by 12 per cent. Even in play, it seems that practice makes perfect – if one has the right temperament and style.

Making things happen

Perhaps the greatest dilemma and most difficult practical skill facing those who look after young children is working out how to make things happen which the children will find interesting and rewarding without, at the same time, over-controlling things and taking the essential spontaneity of children's experiences away from them. On the one hand, does one leave the isolated, under-reactive child alone, or help him join in with others? Does one attempt to try and steer the over-frenetic child into a period of quieter, more concentrated activity? More deeply, how does one help pass on to the child knowledge about others and the world he lives in? Can he possibly be expected to discover, alone, all the complexities of life, acquiring them naturally through his commerce with nature and his peers? The young child still faces many difficulties in empathizing with others and working with them. Can one child, sharing the same stages of growth, possibly provide his peers with the sort of sensitive, contingent framework they need, say, to hold sustained conversations about their own experiences or those of others? How far is it the practitioners' job to help the children along in the development of these personal abilities and is it at all possible to achieve the many objectives they set for themselves without involving themselves in such activities?

The worry that our practitioners felt about stage managing contrived interactions with children (which they probably share with the majority of those who work with preschoolers) has a good deal of weight. Their intuition that it is best to work out from the child's spontaneous interest and involvement has much to recommend it. However, we feel that waiting for nature is not enough. If the adult constantly floats by, or is continually on the move, not seeking extended interactions with children, she will tend to be pulled into managerial activity and engaged in rather disjointed, superficial encounters. These, given the problems of working with groups of children and the children's own stage of development, will tend to lead her into a pattern of working which closes her ears to children's own attempts at sustained interaction, as we saw in Chapter 4. If the goal of working on a one-to-one basis with a child is not seen as an important part of the practitioner's task, then the rather diffuse aim of waiting for a child's interest and catching it at the right moment is unlikely to be met. On the other hand, with children of this age, a more didactic approach, with its risk of too many adult questions, or questions out of phase with the child's immediate interest and superficial questions to which the adult already knows the answer, is also a real danger. Setting out to cause worthwhile experiences for the child runs the risk of falling into the didactic trap. We argued in Chapter 1 that children do not come to their first experiences of public life equally armed to take advantage of what they encounter and the opportunities offered. Children already pre-disposed only to use the adult as a managerial device – as indicated in Turner's (1977) study – are surely likely to continue in this mould when they meet adults continually on the hoof. Nature does not always take care of its own.

The stage at which these young children are – their still limited experience in dialogue with relative strangers and their rather pre-emptive way of entering interactions – together with the fact that adult and child often do not share a great deal of community knowledge, act to make the role of the practitioner an extremely difficult one. With such problems facing those who try to get the child involved with them in extended and interesting conversation, it is understandable that adults try to make most of the running by asking questions. However, our data also suggest ways in which practitioners might be helped to overcome these difficulties. The common range of topics that figure so prominently in the conversations with preschoolers suggests things that the adult can try to talk about, with a good chance that the child will be interested and active. And a child-centered approach to talk should not be taken to mean only talk about the child himself. To be sure, it seems that topics raised should build on the child's own personal experience and knowledge, but within this framework the adult should not be afraid to talk about herself or reveal her own thoughts. In play and instruction too, the secret seems to be not always to ask the child what he should be or is doing or experiencing, or to turn him back on his own resources, but to encourage a sense of shared quest, in which both adult and child participate actively in the experience. The quality of sharing should be signalled by the adult's readiness to express interest, surprise and suggestions as to what is going on.

We are arguing, then, that the path to effective interactions lies in a contingent response to the child. Adult language and actions should be keyed in as far as possible to his thoughts and actions, but these can be magnified, developed and extended if the adult is prepared to build on them and expose her own ideas.

9

The child-centred adult

Gathering young children in groups, before the age of five, under the care of relative strangers, is a new experiment in social engineering. Its success rests on the capacities of both trained and untrained women to provide children with experiences that they will enjoy, that will promote social and mental well-being, and that will generally serve them well in their later development. Success rests too on the capacity of society at large to provide the right kind of material and environmental circumstances, so that those entrusted with the task of early child care can work effectively and productively in the service of their charges. Above all, perhaps, success and well-being rest on the quality of the *fit* between the needs and potentialities of young children and the human and physical environment in which they are expected to prosper.

To start any discussion of success then, we need insights into the capacities and abilities of the young; knowledge of the aims and aspirations of those who do the caring, and some sense as to how these aims are translated into the ways and means of achievement. Finally, we need to know what social and institutional structures, what materials and environmental designs, promote or impede the fulfilment of those means that work best in the pursuit of the goals that are most relevant and useful in promoting the growth of the young.

These demands are stated easily within a paragraph of print; but their fulfilment, the achievement of a theory and practice of child care through either wisdom or research, is an immense task. For in addition to ideological and theoretical arguments about the needs of children and the essentially political issue as to what constitutes the ideal man and, hence, the proper 'father to man', there are formidable problems in simply finding out how practitioners work, what they strive for, and how far they manage to achieve their own objectives.

There are doubtless many ways in which a society can set about the task of finding out whether its provisions for the young are effective in promoting the development of its children; provisions that will prepare them for healthy, happy and productive membership of the culture of which they will eventually take possession. But there will surely be no scientific answers for such questions – we will never replace our hopes and our intuitions entirely by formulae and theories. In the last analysis, all our futures are so uncertain, the shape of our evolving world so poorly envisaged, that however we arm our children to tackle that future, we can never be sure about the appropriateness of what we are doing.

Because we were not in the job of promoting any particular image of the young child or theory of how he should be led towards maturity, we adopted a research strategy which, we hoped, would help us to discover the aims, aspirations and methods of those who were actually entrusted with the task of working with the young. Although our descriptions and analyses were often a reflection of the ideas and findings derived from psychological research – particularly our analysis of the domains and topics of language and our concern with the contingency of the adults' responses to the children – any evaluation of what occurred on a transcript and any chosen direction for change on the experimental tapes was largely the decision of the practitioners themselves. It was *their* reaction to their own experiences, reflected back to them by our recordings and analyses – that formed the principal basis for any change.

In this chapter, we step back from the detailed findings of our work to consider some of the wider theoretical, practical and political implications which arise out of them. In trying to do this, however, we attempt to keep as far as possible within the practitioner's own sense of what preschool care is about. We have chosen the title for this chapter 'The child-centred adult' as a focus around which to organize and interpret some of our findings because we feel that this best reflects the practitioners' aspirations for themselves – *they* strive towards child-centredness. The term is of course already weighed down with many different interpretations, but we try here to provide a definition of it that is consistent with the aims and practices displayed by our 24 practitioners.

The issues we shall consider revolve around the general question – what does it mean to be child-centred in the context of group care of the under-fives? What image of childhood is that based upon, what philosophies of care does it lead to, and what styles of adult behaviour arise out of it? What characteristics of the young child constrain the workings of the adult and set goals and boundaries for her? What environmental factors help to determine her ability to achieve her ends, and how good is the fit between her style of working and the achievement of 'child-centred' care? When in fact is an adult being child-centred?

In trying to provide some answers to these questions, we will also draw upon research findings from elsewhere, to see how far the very detailed processes and practices of adult work that we have been concerned with help us to understand some of the more general effects that others have found in examining preschool care.

Child-centredness

In all the activities we have observed taking place between practitioners and under-fives we have stressed the central importance of the framework supplied by the adult within which the child works and plays. Even in management, we found marked differences in style between enabling, directive and responsive management. But particularly in conversation, play and instruction, we found that the competence displayed by the young rested on the adult's style of working. At best, a preschool group's environment, layout and pattern of work-sharing between adults, breeds extended, contingent interactions between practitioner and child. It enables the preschooler to bring off a difficult task, to play or talk about his ideas and experience in a way that reflects the very limits of his developing competence. The adult is a primary ingredient in preschool care, the major resource. Through good husbandry and management, she brings children together not only with materials and equipment that help promote their physical, intellectual and emotional well-being, with peers who help each other in the development of social awareness and a sense of the needs of others, but also with herself, thus nurturing the children's emerging abilities.

We should underline again that we are not denying the importance of a child's home background, native abilities or involvement with objects and peers. Common sense, in company with a good deal of empirical evidence, makes it clear that all these things are important and do play a part in forming personality and intelligence. Indeed, working alongside practitioners with their own children, we very readily acknowledged the developmental limitations of under-fives that placed fundamental constraints on what an adult could readily achieve with them. But we argue too that the young child's rather systematic response to the adult's various overtures, coupled with the extremely variable responses which he in turn may meet from adults, demonstrates that it must be the adult who is responsible for how interactions with a child develop and for the level of competence he displays in his dealings with her. While his social background and basic capacities do set limits on what can be achieved at any moment in his preschool life, within these there is a good deal of scope for facilitating or impeding his progress towards greater competence and power.

The sister study which paralleled our work, performed by Sylva and her colleagues, helps to identify some of the benefits, rewards and pleasures that young children gain from their interactions with each other. Bringing children together at this stage in their development provides them with opportunities not only to enjoy each other but also to start the task of creating the social structure within which they will eventually work together and into which they will bring children of their own. Other work, by Smith and his colleagues, for example, also testifies to the tremendous importance of young children's play (e.g. Smith and Dutton, 1979). Supplementing the intense, demanding relationships born of the nuclear family with a 'company of peers' is an experiment that has already proved its worth.

But the young child also needs and enjoys contacts with skilful adults. Sylva's study showed how children often display their most creative and concentrated activities in company with practitioners. Our work adds to this by underlining the importance of dyadic encounters between adult and child, or interactions where only the adult and a very small number of children are involved. We have also identified or inferred some of the factors that facilitate or prevent such encounters in play, conversation and instruction. The first, clearly, is the actual ratio of adults to children. Obviously, if we reject the view that children can derive all they need for full and healthy development at this stage from their dealings with objects and peers, then providing enough adult resources to give the sustained, individual attention that effective conversation, teaching and play demand, becomes a high priority. The adult 'on the hoof', constantly meeting the pressures of managing materials and equipment in the service of groups of children, cannot tune into the individual child for long enough to work out what he is doing, thinking or feeling. And as we have seen, unless she is able to create her conversations around his experiences, past and present, or gear her instruction to his current level of competence at the task in question, her interactions are likely to be set at too low or too high a level. She can only be contingent when she has enough knowledge of the individual child and his ways. Where she lacks it, she is likely to become programmatic in her approach, filling gaps in the interaction with questions and demands of her own. Or she will float by, attending to each and every opening and demand from children, but seldom achieving any depth in her dealings with them.

The teacher or playgroup worker is unlikely to achieve that depth in her contacts with children where her time and energy are in short supply, or where she has been cast into the role of manager. This points to the essential weaknesses of the nursery class, where one teacher, with perhaps a single assistant, is expected to provide for a large number of children. The role of manager is likely to fall on the shoulders of the senior partner; she will find herself facing ever-increasing demands from the children that she *does* act as manager and not as helper, teacher or playmate. The answer to the problem of scarce human resources cannot rest in an overly organized curriculum, based on children acting in concert and in groups. Children at this age are still quite limited in their ability to comprehend or show interest in extended thought or talk about experiences removed from their own activities or home life. Stories and dramas have their part in the preschool day, but furthering a child's thinking, language and imagination also rests on interactions in which his perceptions, memories and future hopes are the topic of attention. Our experiences in making the experimental tapes underlined the tremendous problems that the adult faces in engineering particular types of interaction with children. If the adult's overtures come from 'too far away', if they are not sufficiently locked into the child's immediate concerns, and if conversations do not start and develop from something that is a part of the child's own experiences, then both adult and child face difficulty. The adult is led to initiate and maintain the interactions through questions and control; the child finds himself cast, often rather reluctantly, into the role of respondent.

So there is clearly a need for adult time; time to observe children and work out what their cares and interests are. We should not be bullied by political proclamations about the proper level or provision of teacher resources for the young child. Our yardstick should not be some politically or economically expedient half-truth based on a convenient theory, but one based in actual observations of the quality, depth and extent of contacts between individual children and responsive adults in different situations.

In the present economic climate, however, calls for proper care of the young, or for the adult resources they need for effective development, are unlikely to meet with action, or even approval. So the answer, in the short term at least, has to lie in good management of resources, the construction of preschool environments that buffer adult and child from noise and distraction and, perhaps above all, in the recruitment of parents as colleagues in the preschool enterprise (Smith, 1980).

We discovered quite early on in our research – when working with the three practitioners introduced in Chapter 2 – a basic weakness in our approach. It seemed extremely likely on the basis of our discussions – particularly with Janet whose extremely articulate account of her 'givens' and the way these constrained her opportunities for contact with children – that the physical design of the preschool and, particularly, its ability to support the philosophy adopted by the practitioner, exerts a considerable influence over the form of interactions between teacher and child. The triangle of school philosophy, school design and number of available adults, provides a powerful structure within which the adult's style of working and the nature of her relationships with children are partly pre-determined. But we did not have the resources nor indeed the skills needed to undertake such a study. We were struck, though, by the dearth of knowledge elsewhere about the nature of these 'triangles' and their effects upon the experience of children. But what evidence there is suggests that the relationship between classroom design and the activities and interactions of adults and children is a strong and important one. One study, for instance, (St J. Neill and Denham, 1977) indicates that open classrooms engender high noise levels, boistrous activity, and rather unproductive encounters between adults and children. Isolated studies like these indicate that the physical structure of the preschool environment does indeed exert an important influence on the role of the practitioner. We still lack the detailed knowledge to be able to answer practitioners' questions about the best way to arrange their own, local facilities. Because of this probably central gap in our information about different school designs and the influence they exert over the relationships between adults and children, our consideration of management was inevitably incomplete. We were unable, for example, to calculate how far a high incidence of management resulted from the demands of children, the personality of the adult or the design of her situation.

However, we did find on our experimental tapes that practitioners were usually quite capable of creating conditions for themselves under which the demands of management were substantially reduced. By sitting down more, avoiding areas of high management demand like the painting corner or the milktable, by finding quiet spots and encouraging one or two children to join them in some activity, adults were able to bring off conversation, instruction, and even play, at will. This, in turn, suggests that given adequate resources none of our group needed to be cast permanently in the role of manager as a result of her personality or philosophy. There was nothing to suggest either that the nature of children, or of the preschool situation in general, rules out the possibility of sustained and often highly elaborate interactions between adults and children. So persistent limitations are more likely to result from the givens of the situation – design, layout, number of adults, and prescribed roles – than in flexibility or skill of the adults themselves.

But the constraints imposed by the number of children and the design of the preschool environment is only one set of factors that contributes to high management. In several of the playgroups we worked with, the adult–child ratios were quite favourable, but still the general level of management, both on our recordings and as measured by our own informal observation of the playgroup at work, was high – certainly higher than the practitioners involved had realized. Yvonne, recall, was a playgroup supervisor who found her tape far too high in management for her own liking. Thinking about her recording and her role in the playgroup, she commented how, with growing experience in the running of playgroups, she had gradually been inducted into the task of supervisor, and how, in the process, it had become increasingly difficult for her to achieve her more substantive goals – particularly that of talking to children. Janet's school adopted a pastoral style which also bred high levels of management. Rebecca's was a 'place' model in which children who came into her territory were her major responsibility. Yvonne's group adopted a 'fire-fighting' approach in which no single adult was allotted specific management of space or children, but simply responded to management demands as they came up – rushing to the scene to help, negotiate or direct.

Yvonne herself pin-pointed a potential danger in the generally flexible fire-fighting approach to preschool control. New mothers, coming in their first days to work and help in the preschool, on the lookout for a model of how one behaves in this new environment, look to those with most experience – the supervisors. If these models were continually taking responsibility for the smooth running of things and generally overseeing the children's behaviour, newcomers would tend to follow her lead. Rather than tending to sit down and work with a small group of children, sharing their activities, chatting to them or even involving themselves in their play, they would be continually up on their feet, mobile and generally adopting the supervisory stance if not the role of manager. The practical suggestion to which this leads is simply that groups of adults in charge of children should be made aware of the many different roles and styles of adult work in a preschool. They may not want to go so far as explicitly to divide roles out between themselves – a manager, conversationalist, player or whatever – but they should be aware that if, say, they enjoy sitting down chatting to children about their experiences, they are not 'goofing off' nor wasting time. They need not be on the move all the time, even if the supervisor is. However, as we have also seen, flexibility and contingent responses to children's overtures are also vital. An attempt to share out roles should not, therefore, be taken as an invitation to increase the incidence of adult-led group activities.

We hope that by providing a language to describe the many different facets of work with under-fives and by illustrating the value to children of different types of encounter with adults, we can raise practitioners' awareness of the several options facing them. They should look around to see if they are all constantly on the move, looking for managerial openings. Are some adults, at least, sitting down with groups of children for sustained periods? Are they available to those children who want to solicit conversation or other types of interaction? Are they doing enough actively to integrate the isolated or reluctant child?

Where there are groups of adults available, then, by deliberately considering the whole range of goals and roles that can be filled; by not expecting each new adult to know spontaneously how to behave, it should prove possible to provide the whole spectrum of adult-based activities that children might want to exploit. Other practical suggestions that arose from our recordings and discussions, centre on the questions of timetabled activities. Where there are a good number of these, the day or half day broken up into a variety of distinct activities each allotted its own time, and particularly where children are allowed to choose whether or not they wish to participate, then the path is set for a good deal of management. Wherever there is an extensive change-over time, it will be filled with management requests. Children will be interrupted, adults will be brought to their feet, questions will be asked, directions given and the whole room set in motion. The longer these periods last – as they are likely to, for example, in the pastoral, open school system with free choice – then, clearly, the more the adult will act and be seen by children as a manager. She will create her role through her behaviour towards children whatever her self-image or her wider objectives. Whether a group decides to adopt fewer timetable choice points or elects to make these less optional, is clearly a matter for their choice.

Centring on the 'difficult' child

By looking in so much detail at the activities of adults in preschools, we are aware that our image of the child has become a little blurred and indistinct. We have not had detailed background information about the children involved in the different playgroups and nursery schools and, in consequence, we have not been able to ascertain how far each adult's style of working is influenced by the nature of the children in her charge. We have no doubt at all that differences between children do indeed exert their influence on the adult's way of working, just as her way of working acts back, in turn, on them. It is the complex, reciprocal interplay between adults and children that creates the overall 'feel' or climate of each group. In this section, we examine the relationships between our adult-focused work and other research that has looked in more detail at the responses of individual children to their preschool experiences and, in particular, at the way that the child's home background influences the behaviour of teachers and other practitioners towards him. We mentioned such research in Chapter 1. Here we return to consider the insights to be gained by putting our work and these together.

It comes as no surprise to find research showing that the preschool experience means different things to different children. It appeals to one of our common senses. It is self-apparent that children differ in their personalities, aptitudes, likes and dislikes, and it is hardly surprising that these differences are reflected in what they make of and take from their life in preschool groups. However, what is more important about such research is its suggestion that the impact on different children is dependent not only upon idiosyncrasies of each child, but also in part, upon more general social factors reflected in the child's home background. Tizard and her colleagues found that children's responses to life in nursery school differed in a number of respects according to social background – but that the differences were not nearly so marked when they were observed in their own homes. Working-class children were less likely to approach their teachers to solicit interaction, but were more likely to come for services and management. They were rarely seen in extended conversation with teacher, asked fewer questions of her and, in general, were involved infrequently in contingent, reciprocal interactions. But in their home environments, the same children tended to ask mum questions, hold extended exchanges and generally interact as frequently as the middle-class children. Seeing the two groups of children in school alone, noticing, perhaps, the rather managerial encounters between some children and teachers, and the more extended interactions between others, one might be tempted to explain the difference by home background alone. One might even conclude that some children are linguistically or culturally disadvantaged. For Tizard's group of working-class girls (who it should be noted came from stable, two-parent families) such conclusions are unsound. Whatever caused the different quality of relationships between working-class and middle-class children and their teachers, it was not any obvious social or linguistic deficiencies in the children's backgrounds. This conclusion from Tizard's study is echoed in a number of other recent studies, and we can perhaps safely conclude that there is no weakness in children from working-class backgrounds which explains why they respond so differently and, eventually, achieve less in the educational system generally.

Turner, in another study mentioned, also found marked differences in the way that playgroup workers responded to young children. In short, adults were more likely to become enmeshed in managerial encounters with some children and social interactions with others. But the really important finding that Turner reported was an association between the frequency with which an adult managed a particular child and that child's level of linguistic abilities measured by tests. It is tempting to accept the suggestion that the adult's tendency to manage rather than interact with such children was somehow responsible for the rates of language development. We could even tie in our observations of the language of the preschool with this conclusion. The language of management, recall, was highly context-dependent. It offered the child no real opportunities for extended, demanding, interesting use of language, memory or thought. It would be plausible to suppose that the difference in the language environment provided by adults in talking to different 'types' of children helps to create the children's different language achievements. But our own results suggest that the relationship between adult and child is far more complex than this.

In the first place, it seems likely that the child who is managed more perceives the strange adult in different ways. If this is the case, any attempt to measure his language ability in a test is beset with problems. He may well be reluctant to play the tester's game – if he does not readily solicit interactions with those who look after him in the preschool he is unlikely to appear at his most competent faced with a strange tester. So his test results may not properly reflect his level of language ability. As Tizard's study shows, differences which appear between children, their language and their use of the adult in the preschool cannot be taken as evidence of general differences between children.

How, then, can we account for the fact that children approach adults for different purposes and that some show different levels of apparent competence at home and school? As we have already pointed out, it is a major weakness of our study that we did not have any systematic information about the children who took part in the study. Only the consistency with which children in general responded to particular adults gave us confidence that the styles of adult behaviour we have identified do have general effects. Programmatic styles, for example, tend to breed reluctant offerings from children in general while contingent styles are more likely to bring off sustained and interesting interactions. But, as we saw in Chapter 4, one important factor that influences the adult's ability to start and maintain conversations with young children is the extent of her background knowledge of the child. Where there is a good deal of shared, community knowledge conversations were relatively easy to maintain – where there is not, there is a much greater chance of a programmatic approach. This leads us to ask whether the differences reported by Tizard, Turner and others showing quite different responses of children from different backgrounds, might not stem in part from such differences in background knowledge, expectations and experiences of some children and the adults who look after them. Perhaps the child from a middle-class background is more readily understood by teachers and playgroup workers than a child from a different social background?

Another feature of Tizard's results sheds light on the possible reasons why some children are more difficult to centre on than others. She reports that although children from different social backgrounds were all involved in a great deal of interactions with mum at home, the children from working-class backgrounds were more likely to meet with a controlling style from their mothers. In our terms, their actions were managed more. At school, they were also taught more didactically – they met a greater frequency of questions from teacher than their middle-class peers. If the child is managed more at home, perhaps this helps shape his orientation towards adults – he comes to them expecting management and control. What we are suggesting, then, is that where mothers bring different styles of control and interaction to their children, the children carry this expectation over to other adults in the preschool. Thus, the differences lie not so much in the language of the child, as they do upon the patterns of control and teaching that he meets at home.

We obviously have no evidence for these speculations derived from the work reported in this book, but a number of other studies have pointed to similar differences in maternal styles and one experimental study, by Hartmaan and Haavind (1977), has shown that when a child meets with a new teacher the way he responds to her reflects his characteristic style of working with his mother. Children of mothers who adopt a very controlling style with them, for example, who tell them what to do, seldom explain the principles of what they are doing or why, and fail to give them a clearly articulated framework within which to operate, respond rather passively when faced with the strange adult. They tend to wait to be told what to do, seldom ask questions or demand reasons. On the other hand, children of mothers who explain what they should do and why, who invite them to consider certain lines of action rather than just tell them what to do, *do* ask questions and solicit reasons of a strange teacher, and do tell her what they are doing and why.

It is possible, of course, that a mother's style itself reflects a passive or active child and does not 'cause' one. Some researchers have suggested, in fact, that talking about cause and effect in this context is too simple-minded. They suggest that children's lives in different sub-cultures are so different that they actually need to learn different styles of adjustment as their environment changes from that of their parents. Life in a crowded urban environment, for example, where adults and children are locked in cramped surroundings, is likely to demand quite different styles of living from that in a spacious, safer rural setting where adult and child have room to move around without the constant threat of danger and so forth.

There is no good reason at present to rule out any of these factors. They are all plausible candidates for major influences on the developing child. Does that mean, then, that the preschool practitioner is powerless in the face of marked differences between children? The answer, in short, is 'no'. In the first place, as we saw in Chapter 1, there have been successful attempts to improve the educational lot of children from economically poor backgrounds. These suggest that success lies in protracted support for the child and depends on an influence upon the social framework of his life, particularly an influence on parents. And more detailed though less extensive studies in the classroom and laboratory point in a similar direction. Where researchers have imitated the teaching styles of different teachers or mothers and have then gone on to teach randomly selected groups of children using those same styles, they have met with effects on the new children similar to those discovered initially between mother and child (e.g. Wood, Wood and Middleton, 1978; Nuthall and Church, 1973). In other words, when we imitate the style of a contingent mother, for example, and teach other children contingently, they learn relatively easily. When we imitate other, less contingent styles, the children taught do less well.

All this suggests, then, that while it may be more difficult for a practitioner to get on to the same wave length with some children than others, once they have got a child going – perhaps by working alongside him as we suggested in Chapter 6, playing with him or talking to him about the topics of conversation discussed in Chapter 5 – if they go on to provide a contingent, enabling framework, they will help him appear at his most competent.

It may be more difficult to interest and involve some children in interactions not so much because they lack any basic competence linguistically or otherwise, then, but because their perception of the situation and of the adult is quite different. However, when the adult takes the child's interest and ideas as a focus and maintains the interaction contingently rather than programmatically his competence may begin to show through.

To the teacher or playgroup worker who wants to engage all the children in sustained, elaborate interactions, the only practical advice we can give is to start from the child's own experiences – his home, holidays, toys, family, and so on. Avoid a didactic approach, don't resort to questions which violate the normal rules of discourse – 'What colour's your frock?' Do tell the child about yourself, and explain your own views, intentions and experiences. We are not, of course advocating a system which has the adult continually 'on the child's back'. The proper deployment of adult resources is a much more subtle affair, and achieves a blend of free interaction between child, materials, other children and adults. Our practitioners, certainly, did not see their primary role as that of teacher in any formal sense, and were extremely reluctant to force their attentions upon any child. But they did generally recognize the importance and value of interactions built upon the child's own spontaneous offerings. The problem to bear in mind is that children who are unlikely to appear at their most competent in the preschool are those who are least likely to initiate such contacts spontaneously. We must ask ourselves whether we may not have to be a litttle more deliberate and selective in our approaches towards young children. If the goal is to enable all the children to take advantage of the opportunities offered in the preschool, there is groundwork to do with some of them, to help them see opportunities which, initially, they may not realize exist at all. Their perception of the adult is not the adult's perception of herself. Their view of the scope of opportunities offered by the playgroup or nursery school is more limited than the practitioner's. To achieve child-centredness with some children, then, requires more than waiting for the child's initiative. The adult has to show that they are available for more than routine management and are prepared to talk, play and help.

Is training the way forward?

Playgroups seem to be here to stay. Given the present political climate it is not clear that many nursery schools are. Where government seems to have given up any intention or even aspiration to provide proper care and education for the children of women at work, the future which seems most likely and desirable is some form of full day care on the lines of our current playgroups. Where nursery schools manage to survive at all, perhaps their brightest future lies in an active involvement of some parents, since it seems highly unlikely that any more resources are going to be made available by the State.

But if we are going to hand our children over into more extensive preschool care, whether in playgroups or in nursery schools with a complement of untrained parents, is there a need to set up any formal machinery for training those who do the caring? And who should decide what and how training should take place? Happily, since the State seems unlikely to increase its investment in preschool care, it is also unlikely to get involved in the decision making process. But what about the volunteer organizations like the PPA – should they perhaps, be more involved in training and in passing on accumulated knowledge as to how to run groups of children in playgroups? They already have an infrastructure of advisers who are available to help playgroups get started and run effectively. Should they be increasing and developing their ability to pass on their knowledge?

This is a sensitive question. On the one hand, there is recognition that experience is worth passing on and sharing and that preschool care is not a natural extension of mothering. The content of *Contact*, the PPA's magazine illustrates a wide-ranging knowledge of child development and the effective ways of fostering it. But is there a need to do more – and, if so, more what?

Certainly, there is nothing in our findings to suggest that any central curriculum, to be followed by all groups, would be at all a good thing. We have constantly been struck in our recordings by the essentially everyday nature of the interactions between adults and children. Many of our practitioners, trained and untrained, seemed to home in spontaneously on what interested children and to carry them forward. The development of children at this age seems so intimately tied up with their own practical experiences that any attempt to introduce a generalized programme or package would plainly be inadvisable. The present concern of those who look after young children, to stay centred on the individual child, his interests, memories, hopes and thoughts, has a good deal to recommend it.

On the other hand, our observations did make another point. We know that management often rises to unacceptable levels in preschools, detracting from the more substantive task of integrating with children on a personal basis.

From other studies, we also know that some children are not likely to derive as much benefit from contacts with adults as they might. The practitioner's attempts to engage children in conversation, play and shared activity is often threatened, then, both by the nature of her relationships with some children and a general pull towards management. We also found that practitioners often did not 'know themselves' in the sense that they were surprised by what they found themselves doing on our recordings. There was a gap between their aspirations and behaviour, a gap which usually took the form of ignoring overtures from children, asking them too many, often unnatural questions, and not giving them enough time to put their own ideas, words or intentions into action. All this suggests that there *is* scope for some form of training or preparation for preschool care. Certainly, discussions about how to manage, which already take place, need to be amplified by discussions of work sharing.

We have also identified some of the problems that practitioners face in trying to work with young children. We have seen how, in the face of such difficulties, practitioners may be forced into styles of working with children which essentially defeat their own objectives. We have, we believe, illustrated some of the features of adult style that help overcome these problems.

The complexities and difficulties of preschool care need to be articulated clearly in the hope that raising consciousness about common troubles will lead to systematic attempts to ameliorate or overcome them. Given the tremendous importance of local conditions – school design, the group's philosophy and the backgrounds of the children – there are probably no universal *answers* to the problems. But there will be much to be shared by way of approaches and ideas – always accepting that while the problems may be common ones the solutions probably will not be.

What is called for, then, is an open-minded, exploratory attitude on the part of those who set up and maintain centres of care. They rightly avoid falling into the trap of supposing that a common formula exists for all preschool working – but this should not detract from the fact that there may be common difficulties to be overcome. The explicit recognition of these problems would in itself be a major step. A newcomer to the preschool scene, armed with a knowledge of the problems of management, work-sharing, community knowledge, self-defeating questions, and the like, may well train herself into the task of working with under-fives.

Linnet McMahon and Yvonne Cranstoun, are now actively working on this problem in the wake of the OPRG. They are continuing to experiment with the documentary techniques and also trying new methods – providing people with examples of a range of styles and techniques derived from our recordings to see whether it is possible to raise practitioners' awareness and help them train themselves without the laborious and often threatening processes that our 24 put themselves through (see Appendix A).

Whether it is possible to make a rather objective, deliberate attempt to pass on knowledge and techniques to those who follow on and perpetuate preschool care, without destroying the 'local texture' and the natural zest of those who do the caring, remains to be seen. We hope that the attempts reported here will serve to complement the innovation and intuition which currently typifies preschool care. We hope we have underlined often enough our aspirations not to push such intuitions into barren theory and arid 'programmes'. Practitioners, like their children, should not only work in the preschool – they must enjoy it too.

Appendix A

Using transcripts and coding systems for group dissemination

Two playgroup training days

The Social Services Playgroup Adviser for the Abingdon and Wantage areas of Berkshire, holds a training day for playgroup workers once a term. She had asked what the OPRG could offer for a training day and had chosen from the suggestions offered a session on how playgroup staff use their time, based on the 'target teacher' tape recordings. The session was called 'Looking at ourselves at work!' This became the blueprint for group dissemination practice.

We shared two sessions in December 1977, one session in Abingdon and one in Grove. Each session was divided, roughly, into discussion of (1) what the adult does and how she perceives her role, and (2) how to hold a successful conversation with children.

1 What the Adult does

We introduced our handout 'Two ways of thinking about and talking to children' and discussed who starts a conversation (whether it is the adult or the child), and what the conversation is about – either management (constructive, destructive or just management) or interaction (conversation, teaching or play). We described what we can learn from this – how the adult sees her job, how the child sees the adult, and whether their views of each other coincide.

Then we introduced several transcripts (excerpts from tape recordings) which were discussed in small groups at first, and then by the whole group. We asked members to look at the transcripts to find that was 'management' and what was 'interaction', to see if the management were successful; if not, why not? How else could it be done?

One transcript was about organizing and helping different children and so eventually freeing the adult to make a requested pretend visit as 'granny' to a child in the home corner (Transcript A). Another was on turn-taking (B). The third, which provoked most discussion, was milk-time, a session when the adult's intention was to hold a conversation with the children. Which worked better, a group milk-time or a cafeteria system? Much depended on one's aims. Interaction with adults was best in small groups, and maybe even better at other times because children often saw milk-time simply as a chance for rest and relaxation from play, and preferred silence. Some saw a cafeteria milk-time as better without an adult – the children could pour their own milk and enjoyed talking to each other. But it can be difficult for a less articulate child to enter the conversation where there is no supporting adult. Some saw milk-time as a time to come together as a group (though we warned of the danger of children having to waste time sitting waiting in silence) and as a chance for social interchange.

If milk-time were not always the ideal occasion for conversation, we discussed the need to provide other opportunities for this. Should there be a special time? a special place? (such as the book corner) a special adult? (most felt that an adult who saw her job as 'the conversation person' would be too self-conscious: conversation often stemmed from 'mothering' services provided) or a special child? (We mentioned Cazden's (1977) finding that the children who most need conversation received least, as they are hard to talk to, are unrewarding and don't approach adults.) There was discussion of the playgroup time-table and routines but perhaps less than we had hoped on work-sharing in the playgroup – (who does what? where? standing or sitting down? what about mutual back-up?)

2 How to talk to children successfully

We introduced the second part of our handout, 'What is the adult talking about?' and briefly looked at topics and domains. We described which ones appeared to be most common, and explained why we thought it was valuable to explore different domains – helping the child reflect, organize and express his thoughts, helping the development of abstract thought. We used Transcript D 'Grandpy's wedding', to illustrate domains and topics.

We stressed the importance of looking at the child's response to the adult. Which topics lead the child on in his thought and conversation and which produce a brief 'closed' response? Examples of the latter are questions about colour and number, 'What colour is this?', 'How many bricks are there?'. I think this may have fallen on fertile ground, as many playgroup people think these *are* the sort of questions they should be asking! From this, we talked about the importance of the child not thinking you already knew the answer. (You *could* ask, 'What colour is your car at home?') Yet playgroup people have an advantage in talking about other times and places because they often know the child's home and neighbourhood.

We used Transcript E 'Puss in Boots', together with the actual audio tapes that it had been transcribed from to highlight aspects of interactions which were not apparent in the transcript, such as tone of voice and the time allowed for a child to respond. We asked members to try and pick out the skills of the adult in holding a conversation – what were they talking about; who made the opening move; how the adult asked questions; how the child's responses were followed up. This was a difficult exercise but seemed very valuable, especially when we looked in detail at small sections of conversation. We could have been even more precise and detailed in our attention to this.

The kinds of propositions and skills that were discussed included:

1 The subject should relate directly to the child and his experience (only talk about others if the child raises them).
2 Conversation, with mutual respect and enjoyment between adult and child, is better than 'teaching' (where the child knows that teacher knows the answer).
3 Listening carefully, and taking cue from that.
4 Handing the conversation back to the child each time.
5 Waiting for the child to reply.
6 Modifying or re-phrasing questions if necessary.
7 Avoiding a barrage of questions.
8 A running commentary can be better than questions.

There was also discussion of the use of books and pictures as 'props' for conversation when knowledge of the child was lacking. Some feared the loss of the value of the story itself. It seems that conversation and storytelling should be seen as distinct if related activities. If the supervisor herself could not devote enough time to any one activity, could she structure the session so that some other adult were available for the purpose? Perhaps supervisors could make more use of parents for this; this would also make those parents feel more valued. There was also some discussion of joining in play, particularly pretend play, which was held to be fine as long as one were not directing the play but rather were subtly supporting it (see 'Granny's Visit'). A doll's house or a farm could also be useful as the basis for a pretend conversation between adult and child and where a child lacked ideas, the adult could initiate pretend play. We found it interesting that few of our recordings so far had shown adult involvement in play.

There was brief discussion, less than we intended, perhaps, about other props than books which could be used as the basis for conversation where, for example, one did not know the child or his background. (For instance, serial pictures, ambiguous room pictures). I think most people felt they often needed some prop to stimulate conversation.

We were delighted to hear that this was 'one of our most successful training days'. We were told the technique 'could be used to study ourselves at work in many different ways – in fact we could all benefit from seeing ourselves more accurately . . .'.

Two ways of thinking about 'talking to children'

Who starts a conversation? The initial coding

A conversation may be started by an adult or a child. It ends when the adult addresses or is addressed by another child. Go from who *speaks* first, unless there is a clear indication of an unspoken initiation. (If several children speak and the adult follows up on only one of them, count it as *one* child initiation).

> Underline adult openings in red.
> Underline child openings in green.

Then look more closely at each opening statement. Does it concern *Management or services*? – to do with access to materials, turn-taking, arbitration, getting help (e.g. with a cut finger), getting ready for an activity (e.g. putting on an apron). If so, label it M. Or does it concern *interaction*? the child approaches the adult or the adult the child intending not only to get help with something but for more general conversation. If so, label I. It may be general conversation, exchange of information or an attempt to 'teach' something (Ia), or it may be to do with play, getting involved in or starting a play theme (Ib).

What can we learn from this?

1 How the adult sees her job. Is she a manager, arbiter and provider of services, or is she a talker, teacher or playmate?

2 How the children see the adult. Do they go to her for specific help or to be told what or how to do something, or do they go to her for conversation, discussion and play?
3 Do children's and adult's views of each other coincide?

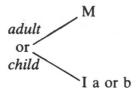

adult
 or
child
   I a or b

What is the adult talking about?

What is each remark of the adult about? After each remark, think about who should, could or would act (or act differently) next, and choose the appropriate one of the following categories.

1 To do with the adult speaking
2 To do with the child
3 To do with other children or adults present (present others)
  e.g. 'It's Peter's turn next.'
4 To do with children or adults who are not there (absent others)
  e.g. 'Does Daddy play music on his (tape recorder)?'
5 To do with rules of behaviour, conventions and why people behave as they do (generalized other – psychological domain)
  e.g. 'We always wash our hands before we eat.'
     'Why is Alison crying?'
6 To do with the logic and nature of events (logical domain – often includes 'because' 'must' 'necessary' 'if' 'then' 'same' 'as')
  e.g. 'They won't stay on (that flat tray) if you turn it over, will they?'

7 To do with imaginary events (the imaginary others – things in the mind only)
   e.g. 'Can I have a sausage on a stick Laura?'
8 To do with groups. The adult is talking to a group of children rather than individuals e.g. at storytime or group discussions.
   e.g. 'Let's turn over the page and see what's about to happen.'
9 To do with labels and properties of objects in the world around
   e.g. 'Is that a vintage car?'

For each category, decide whether it concerns:

The present
The immediate past (earlier in the session – recalled events, promises kept)
The immediate future (later in the session – including promises, plans, threats)
The more distant past (before the session)
The more distant future (after the session)
? other places at unspecified times?

Then look to see how the child responds. Which subjects and which approaches really work?

Granny's visit (A)

A: Have you finished this one Darrel?
C: Oh yes.
A: Do you want to do another one, do you want to do a big one like that? That's alright then. Let's just write your name on this one first. Come and sit down here. Mind you don't get paint on you Sally, can you manage?
C: Eeogh!
A: (aside: trying to hang up her own painting) . . . Very easy. Where shall I write it Darrel, top or bottom?

c: Top?

a: Right, if we do that your hands are going to get wet on the paint, so if I turn it round this way it makes it down at the bottom now, doesn't it? Can you hold the pencil? Oh Sally, I think that Darrel's picture. If you want to use it, Darrel can have another sheet, open it up like that and then you'll have a big piece. (inaudible) There, that's right Darrel. Alright?

c: . . . You have to knock on the door.

a: I've got to come and knock on the door – I'll come in just a moment Esther. Can you jump down? I think I'd better tuck you in Colin, you're coming apart in the middle aren't you? What happened to the trains, did you put them all away?

c: Yes, they fell out. . . . that's why.

a: Who fell out?

c: All the *trains*.

a: Out of the box?

c: No . . . hmm . . . (c2: something about out)

a: Oh well. (sounds of putting away?)

a: Come and have a look at this over here, Simon and Colin, you could play together, couldn't you? Have you done one of these before? Right, you go and find something else then. This is what you have to do, Simon. (Aside: Simon's one of the new children.) Sarah do you want to come and do one? Stand on here, all you have to do is push the nails through the holes with your fingers and then you can put all the different shapes onto the board. Can you get the nails stuck in alright?

c: . . . stuck in.

a: No it won't be able to go on top, they all just have to go flat on the board. Do you want to do that one, Sarah? Take the nails out first and then you can start again (and Katy?) (c: inaudible)

a: Hmm, take them out first.

c: Who's knocking on the door? (?)

a: Hello. I'm your granny, I've come to visit you. (aside: she's making dinner for me.)

c: I've made you dinner.

a: Oh you have, thank you very much.

c: (interrupting) I'm just sitting down.

a: I'm very hungry. Now, there's some lovely dinner here. You've been very busy.

c: Yes, I baked it all . . . I did manage. I've got *all* these babies.

a: You have got a lot of babies, are *the others all asleep*?

c: Yes. 'Cept these.

a: Expect they'd like some dinner too wouldn't they?

c: Yes.

On the beach (B)

a: I think that dog's about to do something.

c1: Jump in and swim.

a: He might.

c: (interrupts) I've never been in here – jump in.

c1: (breaks in) 'Cos they can swim, they just push their paws.

a: That's right, they can, yes. They're very good swimmers.

c1: They go . . .

a: Yes, he *might* just do something to that man.

c: Bump in 'im.

a: He might knock him over.

c1: Yes and he kill (?) him.

a: Look at that . . .

c: (breaks in) Look at him, he's nearly going out far (?).

c1: What's the man (?) doing?

a: What are they about to do?

c1: They're going to swim in.

a: But before they swim what will they have to do?

c1: They jump.

a: I think they're going to dive aren't they? They've got their hands ready, to dive into the water. What do you see there?

c3: A crab.

c: It pick that lady up. (?)

A: Do you think it's going to bite the lady?

c1: Where's the crab?

c: There's the crab! Ha ha! (laughs)

A: Let's turn over the page and see what's about to happen.

c1: Yes. A boy got her.

A: Oh, look, that's all the things that happened. Yes he did fall off. Where did he fall?

c1: On the man.

A: Right on top of the man.

c: (at same time) . . . look.

A: That other little boy, yes. What's he doing?

c1: Holding the boat.

c: O look 'e's fell over.

c3: O look!

Milk-time (C)

A: Here we are, then, here's the milk.

cs (several assertive voices)

A: Would you like to hand me your cup then. Here we are.

c: (inaudible)

A: Sorry Natasha? I can't hear you darling.
Lee, no more chairs out now please. We have enough, thank you.

LEE: Enough.

A: You must wait until someone gets up. We don't have any extra chairs. When someone gets up you can take their place.

c: (inaudible)

A: Now, Natash, you want this yellow one? (?) Right.

c: . . .

LEE: Is that Coke?

c3: I like . . . Coca Cola.

A: No, it's not.
     There we are.
     Now Richard. Oh, Rebecca, that was gone very
     quickly.
     Lee, there's a space round here now if you'd like to
     come and take Rebecca's chair. You are all thirsty
     this morning, hmm? Had a busy morning.

LEE: What's in there? (?)

A: Sorry?

C: That.

A: Oh, that one. That's Ribena. James doesn't drink
     milk, so his mummy brings Ribena for him. Be-
     cause he doesn't drink milk. Is that what you
     thought was Coke?

LEE: Yes.

A: Yes, no it's not, Lee it's . . .

c2: Please can I have some?

Taking turns

c: Yes, but why don't you read this one first?

A: Well, I did promise Andrew I'd read his and then
     I'll read yours next. If you'd like to wait while
     Andrew has his and then I'll read yours Michael. (?)

c1: Oh yes, I'll . . . put it down.

Grandpy's wedding

(READING): 'He gave out his gentle heat and the flowers
            began to open, and the birds began to sing.'
            Look at that lovely bell up in the bell tower.
            There is a bell that rings like that in our
            village. Every time it's one o'clock, or two
            o'clock or three o'clock our bells rings, up in
            our church tower. Do you have one in your
            village?

(Two or three children speak at once)

MICHAEL: I don't live in a village.

A: You do. You live in Tadmarton. That's a village isn't it, Michael?

MICHAEL: Yes, but it doesn't have a bell.

SARAH: I went to a wedding at my church.

A: You went to a wedding at your church, in your village, did you?

SARAH: Yes.

A: Gosh! Whose wedding was that?

SARAH: Not my Mum, but . . . my Grandpy's.

A: Your Grandpy's wedding? How lovely! Where did you sit? (pause) Did you sit down in the church?

SARAH: Well, we didn't go in the church, we went outside.

A: You stayed outside and watched when they came out, did you?

SARAH: Yes.

A: And did he have his wife with him? Did he have the lady he was going to marry with him? . . .

SARAH: Yes.

A: What did they do when they came out?

SARAH: They went back home.

A: They went back home? And did they . . .

SARAH: (breaks in) We took them home.

A: You took them home? In your car?

SARAH: Yes, we brought them.

A: You brought them home. And what did you do when you got home?

SARAH: Well (pause)

A: Did you have a special party?

SARAH: No, we had a picnic outside.

A: A picnic?

SARAH: Yes.

MICHAEL: We had a picnic inside the day after yesterday.

A: You had an inside picnic the day before yesterday, did you?

MICHAEL: Mmm.

A: Where did you have your picnic? Did you spread something out on the carpet or something, and sit on the floor inside?

MICHAEL: Yes.

A: Where did you have it? In your sitting-room?

MICHAEL: Yes.

A: Did you? What did you have to eat?

MICHAEL: Sausages and things, and sandwiches . . .

A: Oh!

MICHAEL: And chocolate biscuits

Puss-in-boots

A: (storytelling again) Then he told some reapers to say that the field they were cutting belonged to the Marquis . . . and they *did* tell the king that, and he was very impressed. They told some more to tell the king the same thing, and they did, and the king was very impressed and thought the Marquis must be very wealthy. Then he went to the castle of a big ogre . . . look how tall he is!

C: Hmm.

A: Do you know anyone that big?

C: Well once we . . . once we saw one, but he shouted at us.

A: You saw an ogre once?

C: No, not a real one, a pretend one. He kept shouting at us.

A: Where was that?

C: That was in . . . Banbury.

A: In Banbury there was a pretend one?

C: He kept shouting at us.

A: What did he (chuckles) shout at you?

c: I've forgotten now.

a: He had a big loud voice, did he?

c: Hmm . . . and . . . and . . . hmm . . . he said *I shall eat* . . . hmm . . . Daddy . . . our Daddy said . . . hmm . . . he, he, he . . . oh, what him!' Daddy said . . . Daddy just said, he said and the giant . . . I said 'would the giant eat us' and daddy said 'if you make a noise it will'.

a: Do you think he would have? (gently)

c: He might just bite us.

a: Didn't you think he was friendly?

c: No . . . he . . .

a: (interrupts) Was he, was he the honey monster?

c: Hmm . . . he was a bit . . . he was a bit shouty.

a: He was a bit noisy, was he? I think I saw him with . . . was he called the honey monster? Was he a great big yellow creature with very big feet that made a lot of noise?

c: My cat's seen the curtains moving while they were drawn.

a: Who saw the curtains moving? You did?

c: No, no, he was hiding behind . . . ? and – and – Jack's mother kept crying.

a: Jack's mother kept crying?

c: Hmm – and there was a pretend cow and the cow was – either – some people?

a: Where was that?

c: That was in Banbury at a show.

a: Oh, you went to a film in Banbury at the cinema, and you saw, you saw all those things happen on the film.

c: An' we saw dalmation dogs.

a: Did you, Matthew?

c: Hmm.

a: You saw *101 Dalmations* . . . what was the . . .

c: (interrupts) Yes and he said we'll feed . . ., and the cow said we'll feed them – and one couldn't reach – one couldn't reach their udder – kept scampering about and it fell off the stool.

A: The puppy fell off?

C: Yes – and and they scampered through the snow – and one kept – to discuss(?) it with us – scared to walk.

A: And did it go out for a walk? Someone take it?

C: Ahmm – eh –

A: Did the puppies have a mummy dog to look after them?

C: And daddy, yes.

A: And a daddy dog?

C: Hmm.

A: Sounds like a nice film. Did you enjoy it?

C: Yes. We're going to Grannie and Pampam's soon.

A: Are you?

C: It's not long now.

A: Where . . . where do they live. A long way away?

C: Yes – in Bristol.

A: In Bristol. You go in the car there, do you? You go and stay overnight there, will you?

C: Sometimes, but we don't usually because, when – we've got Vicky now.

A: Too – it makes too many people in their house does it, when you've got the new baby as well?

C: (interrupts) – because they're old.

A: They're old, oh I see – it's a bit too noisy for them, is it with everybody and the new baby.

C: John and me pull–pull their nose! We like doing that!

A: Do they mind?

C: Only Pampam's, not Grannie's. We've two grannies. One lives with Grandpa and one lives with Pampam.

A: Do they live in the same house?

C: – uhmm – Pampam and Grannie do, and so does Granny with Grandpa live in their house, but, but, not in Pampam's house.

A: They just live nearby, do they, in another house?

C: Just nearby____? but – a bit further away, not very far. There's a zoo in Bristol, isn't there?

A: There is a zoo, yes.

c: Have you been to it?

a: Once, a long time ago when I was a little girl I went to it.

c: Ohh.

a: Do you go to it sometimes when you go to see your grannies?

c: Yes, we might go . . . Daddy said we can go to seaside or the uhh – or the zoo – uhh, when we go there.

a: Oh, that would be lovely. Which do you think you'd rather go to?

c: Ahhmm – the zoo!

a: The zoo. It's nicer than the seaside, is it?

c: Hmm, I think it's nicer. No, I'd like to go to the seaside, first and bring some shells – to Grannie and Pampam, still I brought some for them last time, – might bring some more.

a: 'Spect they were very pleased.

c: Hm, they were.

a: I like to find shells. There are lots of different sorts of shells at the seaside, aren't there?

c: Yes.

a: Different shapes and –

c: (interrupts) – might be a crab or, – or a – hmm – starfish.

a: Might.

c: but these sting, don't they?

a: Uhmm – starfish?

c: Yes – starfish might.

a: (interrupts) Yes, I think they can if you poke them – it's best to leave them alone, isn't it?

c: Hmm. Once I had one in a bucket and I was so scared (it was crawling up) – so, – very carefully, as I was about, I threw it in the sea.

a: 'Spect it would like to be put back in the sea when you'd finished looking at it, wouldn't it?
Oh, did you nail that in, Neville? – that's lovely.

c: It's got some – it's got a nail poking underneath.

A: . . . Very nice.

C: . . . ?

c2: I made – a hole . . .

A: You took it out of the hole, did you?

c2: Yeh – I mean it's on the workbench.

A: Ahh – well it's well in now, isn't it?

c2: Yeh.

A: You'll hammer some more nails in now, are you?

c2: Yeh.

A: Are you?

c2: I got a . . . ?

A: Did you?

c2: Hmm.

(several children's voices in background)

Appendix B
Analysis of Functions

A Problems in coding

With a little practice, most of the functions listed and exemplified in Chapter 3 can be coded quite successfully. We recruited two ex-teachers, neither of whom had been involved in the research, and after 15–20 minutes introduction to the coding system, we asked them both to code two complete transcripts (about 400 events) for function. They achieved a 75 per cent reliability without detailed coaching. The exercise was useful, because the disagreements between these (naïve) coders were rather specific ones and this underlined some problems in what is otherwise a pretty commonsense analysis. After the problems had been identified, each coder was given another ten minutes or so further explanation about the nature of coding and then went on to do more transcripts. On this second run through, they gained 91 per cent reliability on 914 events. The specific problems of coding which this exercise identified are outlined below:

1 Form and function

One problem found was that the coders sometimes confused the form of an utterance with its function. For example, if an adult said to a child 'Would you like to wash your hands, dear?' this question may look like a request for intention (do you want to do X?). However, the hallmark of such requests is that they offer the child a genuine choice: 'Would you like to do another painting?', given the usual free choice in playgroups, is a genuine offer which *can* be refused. However, most management and service 'questions' are usually meant as directions, i.e. *Do* go and wash your hands. Armed with a general knowledge of ethos of playgroups and using the context of an utterance, it is usually relatively easy to achieve consensus about such matters. It is difficult to formalize all the 'rules' we use in reaching such decisions, but people usually agree in their common sense judgements about them.

2 Multiple coding

Many adult utterances towards children involve several functions. For example, where an adult says 'That doesn't look right, get a bigger piece' she is both evaluating and instructing. Similarly, 'That's lovely, do you want to get ready for story now?' is both monitoring and (given context) a management direction.

Usually double coding is straightforward – again, people are able to intuitively break a long utterance down into a set of component functions reliably. However, in some cases the problem is much more difficult. Play, as we saw in Chapter 7, often shades into instruction and conversation – indeed, all three often melt into each other. Thus, when the adult says – 'Oh, he's a coal lorry – what is the coal lorry bringing?' should we count the two utterances as elaborating play or as instruction or conversation? Generally speaking, where there is a clear 'right answer' to the question being asked we would class this as instructional in intent. However, in less obvious cases, we allowed double coding of, say, both instruction and play to mark the ambiguity. There is no simple way of overcoming such basic difficulties with the coding system because we don't have access to the child's perception of the adult's utterance. However, it is possible to reach reasonably reliable judgements by permitting double coding in such cases.

Specific confusions

There were a few quite specific confusions between different categories that we found in the initial run through with the two coders.

Categories 8 and 19 These were sometimes confused. Category 8: Describes/highlights environment – refers to utterances that draw the child's attention to aspects of the ongoing situation and provide some label or description of what he experiences there. Category 19: Gives information – on the other hand, refers to ideas that come directly 'out of the adult's head' – 'It was a lovely day yesterday', 'I really like a hot breakfast', and so forth. Some of the confusion occurred because this distinction was sometimes forgotten by the coders, but at other times it resulted from the fact that we were using audio recordings and it was a matter of judgement as to whether a thing being described or talked about was actually present. With only a sound track to judge by, such confusions are almost bound to occur.

Categories 25 and 26 Repeats and Monitors. There was a small number of differences of opinion concerning these two categories. Since paraphrased repetitions of what the child has just said counted as category 25, it was sometimes the case that the adult's utterance differed by so much from the child's that a coder would judge it to be monitoring rather than repetition. Again, this is a grey area where some confusions are almost bound to occur.

Categories 13 and 19 Evaluates and Gives information. These also led to a number of disagreements. 'That doesn't look right to me', for example, was scored by one coder as evaluation and another as gives information. Again, the best criterion for keeping the two apart is that evaluations are always made of something the child is engaged in. 'Gives information' would be scored where the statement or opinion made was in reference to events/objects/people that could not be seen.

B Statistical analysis of functions in adult activities

Each of the 24 practitioners' transcripts was coded for function and then a rank ordering calculated over the 26 functions. The 24 rank orderings were then compared using Kendall's Test of Concordance (Seigel, 1956). This produced a value of $W = 0.67$. This value is highly significant (Chi Square $= 402$, df $= 25$, $p < 0.001$).

Each adult's functions were grouped into the five categories of instruction, management, conversation, play and rapport. These were converted into percentage scores and then average percentage score over all 24 practitioners was determined. The means and range of percentage scores are listed below:

Management	Instruction	Conversation	Play	Rapport
10·6	27·8	25·4	6·7	29·5
2–44%	6–60%	4–48%	0–73%	9–50%

Functions in adult behaviour and approaches from children – supply and demand

Each time a child approached the practitioner, the reason for contact was classified into two categories – soliciting management (access to turns, equipment, arbitration, services, timetable information) or for interaction (conversational opening, request to play, request to help do or make something or to comment on something achieved etc.). Similarly, the adults' approaches to children were classified into the same two categories. The ratios of interactive/total openings for each practitioner were then rank ordered. Similarly, childrens' openings were expressed in the same way and rank ordered. One tape was so noisy that many openings were obscured and could not be reliably classified. This was rejected from this analysis. One other recording had so few openings (mainly dealing with one, extended adult–child conversation) that a statistical analysis was not feasible. The remaining 22 documentary tapes were rank ordered for both children and practitioner and compared using Siegal's rank-order test of correlation. This yielded a value of $r_s = 0.47$, n = 22, $p < 0.05$. Thus, as we had found in our examination of contacts between Rebecca and her children in comparison with those between children and Janet, adults who approached children for management tended to be approached by children for management; those who solicited interactions met with demands for interaction.

Appendix C
Analysing conversations

A Stages in coding the levels of control in conversations

Recording

A record of the conversation is the obvious first stage and how this is done will depend on how precise an analysis is required. An ordinary tape recording may be sufficient if all participants can be clearly heard and understood. The sooner analysis or transcription occurs after recording the better, because the nuances of interpersonal interaction are difficult to catch on tape and memory of 'how things went' quickly fades. Videotape recording is of course preferable where it is available.

The amount of time recorded will also vary according to requirements. We have usually taken half an hour of conversation on audio or video tapes, which allows for several topics and a number of children to be included. However, if a full written transcript is required, analysis will be excessively time-consuming. Ten minutes is probably sufficient if participants are relaxed, recording is unobtrusive, and precautions taken that what is recorded is fairly 'normal' for the people concerned.

We have mentioned a written transcript – the next stage in research work. Others may only want to make a note of what level of moves are made – perhaps with an occasional note concerning the topic. The tape can then be replayed for further analysis.

B Definition of 'Move'

It was necessary to formulate rules as to what exactly was to be coded as a person's move in a conversation. Adults especially may say several things in between the listener's last and next utterances and it is sometimes difficult to determine what is the essence of the message being put across. In practice it was decided to use the last thing said in a turn. There were two main reasons for this choice. For practical purposes we wished to have a simple adult move – child move – adult move sequence to analyse. Also, when we looked at what the child responded to, it was almost always the last thing the adult had said. So, when we come to look at what the child does in response to certain adult moves – it makes some sense to ignore all but the last utterances. For example:

c:	I went to Goose Fair last night.	(4)
a:	Did you?	(5.2) (see later)
	I love fairs	(4)
	My father used to take me on the big wheel, when I was a child.	(4)
	Did you go on the big wheel?	(2)
c:	Yes.	(√)
a:	You did.	(5)
	and what else did you go on?	(3)
c:	The big roundabout.	(√)

Here both of the child's responses are obviously in answer to the adult's immediately preceding question.

If, however, we ask what is the adult's response to the child – the issue is not as clear. Adults, with their responsibility to 'keep things going' – usually take longer, more complex turns. We might argue that in the example above it is the 'Did you?' and 'You did' which are the adult's responses to the child's utterances. What we have decided however is that we will define the adult's move not in terms of a 'response' but as what she is leading up to in her next demand on the child. Quite often the adult's tone of voice itself suggests that she neither expects nor waits for the child to respond to the earlier utterances (if she does so noticeably – the child is then coded as taking a 'no response' turn). So we again use only the last utterance in our analysis – with possible exceptions happening when there is, for instance, a genuine interruption of the conversation and it is taken up again afresh later.

C Coding categories

Conversation is a dynamic interactive process where language is used creatively to influence another person. We should not therefore expect this language to fall neatly into a small set of categories. What we have devised here is a system which describes most adult–child interactions in conversation – with some exceptions and exclusions already mentioned (see p. 243). As we ourselves have moved from preschool conversations to analyse those between teachers and older deaf children, for example, a few new categories were needed to cover common occurrences (e.g. 'X' to denote child misunderstanding and answering the wrong question). Other groups may also need new categories. Do not classify language into a category where it is obviously in violation of the usual 'force' of that category. A '?' category should be allowed to cover very uncommon moves – so that the coding system does not become too unwieldy. However, if the '?' column becomes large (say greater than 5 per cent of all utterances) you may want to look at it to see if some new factor is suggested.

Levels

The five levels already outlined in Chapter 4 cover most adult moves (and of course such utterances by the child will be coded in the same way).

1 Enforced repetition
2 Closed questions
3 Open questions
4 Contributions
5 Phatics

There are, however, three 'mixtures' of these categories which seemed to warrant a separate category of their own.

5.1: e.g. 'Pardon?' 'What?' 'Eh?' – where there is a mixture of phatic (i.e. I am interested) plus repetition (but of what other has just said, not self).

5.2: e.g. 'Did you?' or 'You went to the fair? (did you)?' where there is a mixture of phatic (repeating others words) plus a closed question. There is a great difference in response from the child between ordinary phatics (you did!) and these 'tag' ones (Did you?) in that the latter allows the child to legitimately answer only with 'yes' for his turn.

4.2: e.g. 'You did have a good time at the fair, didn't you?' where there is a genuine statement which has a tag with similar results to '5.2s'.

Another type of category is e.g. 2/3-utterances which could be construed as a '2' or a '3' – e.g. Do you know what day it is? – the decision here being made in the light of the child's answer.

'OTHER': a dustbin category for 'odd' utterances. Not audible or comprehensible for some reason.

We must now add the more 'responsive' categories.

$\sqrt{}$:   where C appropriately responds to the force of the question and stops (if he is wrong and answers yes for no or blue for red, for example score '$\sqrt{}(x)$' showing an appropriate type of move which is logically incorrect)

$\sqrt{}4$:   where C appropriately answers question and goes on to say something beyond the scope of the question.

nr: no response
x: child misunderstands the whole force of a
           question and for instance says 'yes' to 'where
           did you go?'
x4:   as above plus a contribution of his own
'OTHER':   any utterance which cannot be coded as above
?:   inaudible or incomprehensible

These categories cover the bulk of adult–child conversation and are the only ones used in our further analysis. However the more information that is recorded and coded, the more likely it is that we can pick up on unusual but perhaps significant trends in the way conversations are held. Additional coding has, therefore, been devised as problems have arisen – and is discussed here to illustrate how dilemmas have been dealt with.

D Problems in coding

General principle

If the 'force' of an utterance is unclear, look to what happens before and after – especially at the child's next move. For example, the simple question 'What?' It could be a '5.1', i.e. 'Pardon?' Or it could be a '5.2' – an expression of interest and disbelief. Or, it could be a '3', after e.g. 'I've got something for you'.

The context will usually reveal what the speaker really means by an utterance and the problems that arise are very often due to the fact that in conversation people do not always talk in sentences. Sometimes too, it is a pause plus a questioning expression which must be coded – e.g. 'For your birthday you had a . . .?' with a rising intonation on the 'a', where the intended response is the same as for 'what did you have for your birthday?' If the child's response also agrees with this rephrasing then we can justifiably code this as a '3'.

If, however, this had happened after the child had just said what he'd had for his birthday – the utterance is more likely to be a '5.1' i.e. 'Pardon?'. Similarly with one of the examples mentioned earlier, 'Do you know what day it is?' the child can legitimately answer yes or no, or give the day, e.g. 'Monday'. These would be coded as:

or

A	C		A	C
②/ 3			2 /③	
√(Yes)			√(Monday)	

For further analysis the adult's 'move' would be taken as being a '2' (or a '3') even though we might not want to 'lose' the information that the questions were phrased in this way.

Additional coding

1□:   Some adults do a lot of rephrasing of what the child has said either by expanding it grammatically, or tying two or more of the child's previous utterances together. A straight repetition is of course a '5'. However, if 'Mummy park' is expanded 'Mummy took you to the park, did she? – this is more than the child said (and may in fact not be what he meant at all!). Thus, we need to discriminate this from an ordinary '5.2'. We have so far 'boxed' these utterances '⑤.2' but as yet have done no more about it than that. (Analysis counts this as '5.2'). Where such utterances are numerous, they may demand separate analysis, however. Similarly a '4' can contain a lot of what the child has said – but will become a '④' (as against a '⑤') only when the adult has added some new element and thereby pointed the conversation along slightly new lines.

2.M: Although we have excluded from coding all 'managerial' utterances like 'get your coat on' or 'fetch

a chair' – there remain utterances which are managerial or 'ordering' in tone but still part of conversation proper. For instance:–
'Tell me what you did', is an order but equivalent to 'What did you do?'

Here the presence of 'what' makes it easy to code this as an 'M/ 3.' We must, however, look at the child's reply – for if he answers only – 'No' or 'OK' – then this is a reply to the managerial aspect – which we would then code as 'M → $\sqrt{}$'. For the preschool groups this utterance was then left out of future analyses. When we came to the teachers with deaf pupils, however, where they were more numerous, we decided that we must take them into account. This was mainly due to teachers who, though very low in 'control' in terms of questions, also made great use of 'managed conversation'. We felt these sessions to be 'real conversations' in every sense but frequent instances of certain moves caused problems in coding. Later analysis has shown that children do, in fact, tend to respond differently to these types of moves.

e.g.　(a)　'You ask them if they know what turnips are.'

This resulted in the child addressed answering the question himself – not what the teacher intended. This we finally wrote down as

$$\text{M (3)} \quad \Big| \quad$$
$$\text{X 4 } (\sqrt{})$$

where the M would be analysed as an 'other' move.

(b) 'Are you going to ask her what colour it is?'

This resulted in the child asking the other child 'what colour' (and the other child answering 'blue'). We did not consider this to be just an elaborate '1' nor a '3' despite the 'what' – and settled for

Ⓜ/2 (3)

$\quad$ (√) 3 (to C)

Again the M was analysed as an 'other' move.

In addition to these 'managed conversation' moves, some teachers also do a lot of *ordinary* management of the kind:

> 'Keep quiet, we can't hear what Susan's saying.'

> 'Let's have a look.'

3.√: We have used a '√' to denote an appropriate reply – but of course children do not always obey linguistic rules – and they sometimes get the answer wrong!

√(x): Would denote an appropriate – but wrong – answer (in the light of what comes before or after). For instance they may answer 'yes' instead of 'no', or 'red' instead of 'blue'. They know what type of reply is appropriate but they make a mistake.

(√)4: Has been used in two ways. One is where the child has answered a question, e.g. 'What did you have for your birthday?' – with 'Car', and the adult then gives a 5, e.g. 'Yes' and the child then goes on with a list 'and a bike'. The child could have stopped after one answer – so '√' seems to under-value the following offerings. On the other hand they are not proper '4 s' so the compromise taken was to code these as '(√) 4'.

The second type of '(√) 4' is the case where in answer to a '2', e.g.

'Did you go for a ride in the new car?'   (2)

the child answers –

'It went very fast!'   (√)4

Here the 'yes' is assumed in what he says.

If however he had replied:

'It had to go into the garage',   (4)

we might consider that a 'no' was inherent in the answer – but he might equally well be following up his own theme and ignoring the teacher. In doubtful cases like this we code just a '4'.

4:    So far we have not discriminated between the child's '4s' on the basis of theme – except in relation to the examples mentioned above. These, however, are in response to questions where what one person 'should' answer is laid down by the question. After a '4' or '5' there are no such 'hard rules' of discourse – though some utterances will be seen as more 'polite' or normal for the kind of conversation involved. For instance – it would be 'normal' for one '4' to follow another in the same theme – but it is possible for two people to have parallel conversations – each pursuing his own theme. Between adult and child this rarely happens – as the adult tends to change things – but extreme cases are possible to identify. Again these can be isolated as (4) i.e. where the (4) does not follow on in theme from the other person's '4'. However, genuine interruptions also occur – due to the arrival of a newcomer or to something happening which cannot be identified from the record taken. Again, gestural cues or knowledge of the other's experience may form a 'bridge' between apparently unrelated comments. Such considerations have militated against formal analysis on this point. However, it may be a question to keep in mind if they occur with any regularity.

5:    Ignoring and Interrupting: we have a category 'nr' for 'no response' where a question is followed by a pause which is not 'filled'! Other forms of 'ignoring' are more difficult to pin down – for similar considerations as in (4) above. One problem is

when the child says 'ah . . .' and thinks. We code
this as '5nr'. Whether this is analysed as a '5' or a
'nr' will depend upon the context.

E Summary sheet – levels analysis*

5 Main Levels	–1	Enforced repetition
	2	Closed questions (2 – choice)
	3	Open questions – who, what, where, why, how and so on
	4	Statements and personal contributions
	5	Phatics
Mixtures –	5.1	e.g. 'Pardon?' 'What?'
	5.2	e.g. 'Did you?' or a repetition of child's utterance in question form
	4.2	tag statements '. . ., Didn't you?'
	2/3	e.g. 'Do you know what day it is?'
	*M/3	e.g. 'Tell us what you did.'
	Other	
	?	
Responsive Categories –	√	Appropriate response to a question
	√4	Appropriate response plus a contribution
	nr	No response
	x	Clear misunderstanding
	x4	Clear misunderstanding plus a contribution
	'other'	
	?	Inaudible or incomprehensible

* For more formal school settings, two categories – 'chairing' and 'management' – have been included in analysis where the teacher arranges turn-
taking, people and things to help the conversation run more smoothly.

Other Coding – not used in further analysis.

□	Where adult restates child's utterance
√(x)	Appropriate but wrong (in light of other happenings)
(√)4	Where (√) part is assumed in the answer or a child goes on with a list of things interspersed by e.g. '5s'.

Excluded –	*M	Management of action, e.g. 'Put your apron on'.
	In	Instruction e.g. reading, testing
	Att	Directing attention to materials and so on (unless this is an invitation to converse about them)
	Play	Where the emphasis is on what is being done, with no elaboration.

F The moves matrix

Once the transcript has been coded in terms of adult–child–adult–child moves, the next question is how do children respond to the various types of adult move? – and vice versa.

A simple table answers this question – with adult moves (as on the summary sheet) down one side, child moves along the top (and vice versa for adult responses to children's utterances). Taking each adult move – a felt-tip dot is put into the appropriate 'box' to denote how the child responds.

Calculations
1 The dots are then added up for each 'box'.
2 Horizontal rows of boxes are totalled to give total number of adult moves in each category.

3 Columns of boxes are totalled to give total number of child responses in each category.

4 Percentages of category moves can then be worked out for all categories (from 2 and 3).

5 *Control measures* total percentage adult moves at levels 1, 2, 3 and 5.1, 5.2s and 4.2s. With older children who may not respond to 4.2s and 5.2s as questions as the preschoolers did, it may be worthwhile excluding 4.2s and 5.2s from the control measure.

6 *Child contribution* – total percentage of (a) all 4s. (i.e. 4, $\sqrt{4}$ and 4.2)
(b) (as a) plus 2, 3, 5.2 (i.e. almost all but $\sqrt{}$)

7 *Child contribution in relation to adult move:*
taking each category – e.g. 3s – how often are these responded to (a) with some type of 4? (b) 4s and questions.

8 If applicable, adult control measures can then be correlated with child contribution measures.

G Reliability

Two coders working independently with the same transcripts achieved an overall reliability of 91 per cent (48 disagreements on 509 turns in conversations).

H Major analyses

Since children tend to take single moves most of the time, it follows that adults who ask more 4s or make more 5s also engender more 4s from the child. Those who ask a greater frequency of questions, receive more responses ($\sqrt{}$) but relatively few contributions overall. Thus, when we look at the overall correlations between adult control (all questions) and children's contributions, we find a significant negative correlation ($r = -0.73$, $p < 0.01$, $n = 16$). Thus, because children seldom take double turns, a high incidence of control in adult speech effectively inhibits them from making spontaneous contributions of their own. The opposite pattern is found for the incidence of contributions in adult speech. The rank order correlation between all contributions from children and contributions from the adult was $r = 0.67$, $p < 0.05$, $n = 16$. Since contributions tend to be a stable characteristic of adult style (Chapter 8) this suggests that some adults are generally more likely to provide a conversational framework within which children will readily make contributions.

Of particular interest, is the relationship between adult control and double moves in child speech. Double moves sometimes occur after questions, where the child not only responds to the force of the question but elaborates with a contribution. The correlations between such double moves after questions are generally negatively correlated with the frequency of controlling moves in adult speech, as Table H.1 illustrates.

		Double moves after:		
2	3	4.2	5.2	All questions
−0.62*	−0.45	−0.30	−0.44	−0.54*

* $p < 0.05$, $n = 16$.

Table H.1 *Rank order correlations between adult control and double moves from children*

The most frequent double moves from children occur after closed questions and it is in this context that the correlations between adult control and double moves is most marked.

This analysis suggests, then, that adults who exert a lot of control seldom meet double turns after their questions, those who ask relatively few questions are most likely to receive double turns. Thus, questions both depress the overall frequency of contributions from children and also seem to inhibit double turns from them.

When we look at the pattern of relationships between double turns in child speech and adult contributions, we find the opposite pattern, though none of the comparisons achieves statistical significance.

		Double moves after:		
2	3	4·2	5·2	All questions
0·43	0·17	0·02	0·30	0·30

Table H.2 *Rank order correlations between adult contributions and double moves from children*

Thus, whilst contributions from the teacher are correlated with contributions in child speech, the relationship to double turns is less marked.

H.3 Children's questions When do children ask questions in conversations with practitioners? (n.b. this analysis excludes requests from children which are basically managerial in nature, i.e. access to equipment, turns, arbitration etc.).

In Table H.3 the frequencies with which children asked a question in their turn following each type of (terminal) move from practitioners are listed.

	Terminal move in adult speech							
Percentage followed	2	3	4	5	4·2	5·2	$\sqrt{}$	$\sqrt{4}$
by child question	2	0	10	6	2	3	11	17

Table H.3 *Frequency (percentage) with which each adult move was followed by a question from children*

Generally speaking, children were least likely to include a question in their turn following on any question from the adult. Child questions were relatively most frequent after the least frequent moves in adult speech – i.e. adult's responses to previous questions ($\sqrt{}$,$\sqrt{4}$). Thus, once children had gained control of an adult with a question, they sometimes followed with another question, if the adult simply answered them or answered and elaborated (rather than, say, asking another question of her own). Thus, once in control, children will sometimes stay in control. The other, less controlling moves particularly contributions, also generated a relatively high incidence of questions. A correlation of the sixteen adults' rank order control (all questions) with a rank ordering of questions asked by children on tapes 2 revealed a significant negative correlation ($r = -0.48$, $p < 0.05$). Conversely, there was a significant positive correlation between adult contributions and children's questions ($r = 0.46$, $p < 0.05$). Thus, overall, adults who exert a lot of control seldom meet questions from children, while those who offer personal contributions most often tend to be asked more questions by children. The frequencies of $\sqrt{}$ and $\sqrt{4}$ in adult speech were too small to permit any statistical analyses.

Appendix D
Topics and domains of discourse

A Topics and domains of discourse on documentary tapes

The topics in the speech of each practitioner were rank ordered and the 24 orderings thus achieved subjected to Kendell's test of Concordance. This yielded a value of W = 0·55, Chi Square = 66, df = 5, p < 0·00.. (With references to the 'here-and-now' – the most popular domain – omitted, there was still a residual degree of agreement – W = 0·22, Chi Square = 21, df = 4, p < 0·01.) The same test applied to the rank orderings for topics of discourse gave a value of W = 0·57, Chi Square = 123·12, df = 9, p < 0·00..

B Changes in context dependency and references to the child from tapes 1 and 2

One interest of the study was to see how far practitioners were prepared/able to change the degree of context dependency in their speech to children. The Wilcoxon matched-pairs, signed ranks test was used to compare each practitioner's relative use of the 'here-and-now' domain on the two recordings. Changes in domain away from the here and now averaged 12·2 per cent (T = 35, n = 17, p < 0·05). The proportion of talk about the child being addressed was also compared using the same test. References to the child dropped by a mean 2 per cent but this was not statistically significant (T = 44, n = 15, ns).

An examination of individual changes in relative frequency of usage of both domains and topics, together with changes in control (all questions – including tags) revealed a number of significant changes. Of the 17 practitioners making experimental tapes, only three showed no statistically significant change in topic of conversation and only one no change in domain of discourse. In Table A5.1, the individual patterns of change are listed. In Tables A5.2 and A5.3 the individual increases and decreases in use of each topic and domain are shown.

	Column 1: Topics			Column 2: Domains			Column 3: Questions
Practitioners	Chi Sq.	df	Level	Chi Sq.	df	Level	
1	117·5	5	0·00 . .	51·8	3	0·00 . .	Up 18%
2	59·3	5	0·00 . .	96·3	3	0·00 . .	Up 16%
3	101·1	5	0·00 . .	133·8	3	0·00 . .	Up 2%
4	24·38	5	0·00 . .	201·0	3	0·00 . .	Up 8%
5	121·02	5	0·00 . .	317·1	3	0·00 . .	Up 11%
6	168·0	5	0·00 . .	146·7	3	0·00 , ,	Down 10%
7	55·9	5	0·00 . .	6·95	3	not sig.	Down 18%
8	6·38	5	not sig.	10·1	3	0·02	Up 10%
9	14·14	5	0·02	38·79	3	0·00 . .	Up 9%
10	18·19	5	0·01	27·7	3	0·00 . .	Up 24%
11	91·52	5	0·00 . .	13·65	3	0·01	Up 3%
12	5·3	5	not sig.	8·65	3	0·05	Up 10%
13	13·95	5	0·02	17·5	3	0·01	Down 10%
14	8·54	3	0·05	cell frequencies too small			Up 9%
15	7·58	5	ns	101·5	3	0·00 . .	Up 20%
16	64·3	5	0·00 . .	55·5	3	0·00 . .	Up 3%
17	79·6	5	0·00 . .	118·7	3	0·00 . .	Up 1%

Table A5.1 *Changes in topics, domains and questions from tapes 1 to 2*

Practitioners	Here-and-now	Short-term past and future ⟷	Long-term past and future ⟷	'Timeless'
1	D	D	U	U
2	D	D	U	U
3	D	D	U	U
4	D	U	U	U
5	U	D	D	D
6	U	U	D	D
7	U	O	O	D
8	D	U	U	D
9	D	U	U	U
10	D	U	U	U
11	U	D	D	U
12	D	D	U	U
13	U	U	U	D
14	D	D	U	O
15	D	U	U	U
16	D	D	U	U
17	D	D	U	U
Totals				
Down	12	9	3	5
Up	5	7	13	11
Same	0	1	1	1

D   References go down on tape 2
C   References go up on tape 2
O   No significant change/cells too small for comparison

Table A5.2 *Changes in domains of discourse from tapes 1 to 2*

Changes from Tapes 1 to Tapes 2: Descriptive account.

Practitioners	Child	Objects	Logical	Absent	Imaginary	Pres others
1	D	U	U	U	U	D
2	D	D	U	U	O	D
3	D	U	D	U	U	U
4	O	D	U	U	U	D
5	U	D	D	D	U	O
6	D	D	D	D	U	U
7	O	U	D	U	D	D
8	U	D	U	O*	O	U
9	U	D	U	U	D	U
10	U	U	U	O	D	D
11	D	U	D	U	U	D
12	U	U	D	U	D	D
13	D	U	U	D	U	D
14	U	D	D	O*	D	U
15	O	U	D	U	U	U
16	D	U	D	U	U	D
17	U	D	D	U	D	D
Totals						
Down	7	8	10	3	6	10
Up	7	9	7	11	9	6
Same	3	0	0	3	2	1

* cells too small

D   References go down on tape 2
U   References go up on tape 2
O   No change as too small for overall statistical analysis

Table A5.3 *Changes in topics of discourse from tapes 1 to 2*

C Relative frequencies of personal contributions, phatics and questions in adult speech from tapes 1 to 2

The individual frequencies of adult personal contributions on tapes 1 ranged from 19–40 per cent of all (terminal) moves. On tapes 2 the range was 12–35 per cent. Practitioners were rank ordered in terms of relative frequency of contributions in conversation on the two sets of recordings and these were correlated using Spearman's test to yield a value of $r_s = 0.69$, $n = 16$, $p < 0.01$.

A similar analysis performed on rank order frequencies of both questions ($r_s = 0.01$) and phatics ($r_s = 0.10$) yielded non-significant correlations.

Short bibliography

BANDURA, A. and WALTERS, R. H. (1963) *Social Learning and Personality Development.* New York: Holt, Rinehart and Winston.

BRUNER, J. S. (1966) *Toward a Theory of Instruction.* New York: Norton.

CAZDEN, C. B. (1977) Concentrated versus contrived encounters: Suggestions for language assessment in early childhood education. In Davies, A. (ed.) *Language and Learning in Early Education.* London: Social Science Research Council.

DEPARTMENT OF EDUCATION AND SCIENCE (1972) *Education: a Framework for Expansion.* London: HMSO.

FREYBURG, J. T. (1973) Increasing the imaginative play of urban disadvantaged kindergarten children through systematic training. In Singer, J. L. (ed.) *The Child's World of Make Believe.* London: Academic Press.

HAAVIND, H. and HARTMAN, E. (1977) *Mothers as teachers and their children as learners.* Report No. 1, Institute of Psychology, University of Bergen, Norway.

HOHMANN, M., BANET, B. and WEIKART, D. P. (1979) *Young Children in Action.* Ypsilanti, Michigan: High/Scope.

ISAACS, S. (1936) *Intellectual Growth in Young Children.* London: Routledge.

KARNES, M. B., TESKA, J. A. and HODGINS, A. S. (1970) The effects of four programs of classroom intervention on the intellectual and language development of four-year-old disadvantaged children. *American Journal of Orthopsychiatry,* **40,** 58–76.

LURIA, A. R. and YUDOVICH, F. LA (1971) *Speech and the Development of Mental Processes in the Child.* Penguin papers in education.

MARSHALL, H. R. and HAHN, S. C. (1967) Experimental modification of dramatic play. *Journal of Personality and Social Psychology,* **5,** No. 1, 119–22.

NUTHALL, G. and CHURCH, J. (1973) Experimental studies of teaching behaviour. In Chanan, G. (ed.) *Towards a Science of Teaching.* Slough: National Foundation for Educational Research, 9–25.

RUTTER, M., MAUGHAN, B., MORTIMORE, P. and OUSTON, J. (1979) *Fifteen Thousand Hours: Secondary Schools and their Effects on Children.* London: Open Books; Cambridge, Mass.: Harvard University Press.

SCAIFE, M. and BRUNER, J. S. (1975) The capacity for joint visual attention in the infant. London: *Nature.*

SCHAFFER, H. R. (1977) *Mothering.* London: Open Books/Fontana; Cambridge, Mass.: Harvard University Press.

SMILANSKY, S. (1968) *The Effects of Socio-dramatic Play on Disadvantaged Pre-school Children.* New York: Wiley.

SMITH, P. K. and DUTTON, S. (1979) Play and training in direct and innovative problem solving. *Child Development*, **50**, 830–36.

SNOW, C. E. and FERGUSON, C. A. (eds.) (1977) *Talking to Children.* Cambridge: Cambridge University Press.

SYLVA, K. D., ROY, C. and PAINTER, M. (1980) Childwatching at playgroup and nursery school. London: Grant McIntyre; Ypsilanti, Michigan: High/Scope.

ST. J. NEILL, S. R. and DENHAM, E. (1977) *Psychological Influences of Spatial Design in Nurseries.* Research Report, University of Strathclyde. Departments of Psychology and Architecture.

TAYLOR, P. H., EXON, G. and HOLLEY, B. (1972) *A Study of Nursery Education.* Schools Council Working Paper No. 41. London: Evans Methuen Educational.

TIZARD, J., PERRY, J. and PLEWIS, I. (1976) *All Our Children.* London: Maurice Temple Smith.

TIZARD, B., PHELPS, J., PLEWIS, I. (1976) Staff behaviour in pre-school centres. *Journal of Child Psychology and Psychiatry*, **17**, 21–3.

TIZARD, B., CARMICHAEL, H., HUGHES, M. and PINKERTON, G. (in press) Four year olds talking to mothers and teachers. To appear in *Monographs of the Journal of Child Psychiatry and Psychology.*

TOUGH, J. (1977) *The Development of Meaning.* London: Allen & Unwin.

TURNER, I. F. (1977) Pre-school playgroups research and evaluation project. Final Report submitted to the Government of Northern Ireland Department of Health and Social Services, Department of Psychology, The Queen's University, Belfast.

VYGOTSKY, L. S. (1962) *Thought and Language.* Cambridge, Mass.: MIT Press.

WELLS, C. G. (1978) What makes for success in language development? In Campbell, R. and Smith, P. (eds) *Advances in the Psychology of Language.* New York. Plenum. Vol. III 4a, 449–69.

WOOD, D., BRUNER, J. S. and ROSS, G. (1976) The role of tutoring in problem solving. *Journal of Child Psychology and Psychiatry*, **17**, 2, 89–100.

WOOD, D. J., WOOD, H. A. and MIDDLETON, D. (1978) An experimental evaluation of four face-to-face teaching strategies. *International Journal of Behavioral Development*, **1**, (2), 131–47.

Index

adult functions in preschool, 34, 38–9, 44, 45, 46–8, 179–80, 192–209
control, 50–1, 143–6, 198
conversation, 36–7, 46–8, 50, 182–7
instruction, 35–6, 44, 46, 50, 146, 148, 150
management, 12–13, 18–20, 22–6, 30–2, 35, 41–4, 46–50, 101, 119, 162–3, 192, 195, 198, 201, 202–4
optional activities, 46
play, 36, 44, 46, 48, 50, 126–43, 148, 150–61, 182–7
rapport, 37, 39–41, 46–7, 177
adult-child conversation, control of, 71–81
closed question, 73, 74
contribution, 73, 75
enforced repetition, 73
open question, 73, 75
phatic, 73, 74, 75
adult-child conversation, styles of, 52–5, 82
chaining, 55–61
double turns, 65, 74, 80
fending-off, 64–5, 79, 113–4, 176–7
floating, 62–4
framing, 55–61
motherese, 84
phatic moves, 67–9, 73, 74, 75, 79, 80
programmatic, 65–7, 168, 178, 202–3
silly voice, 116–8, 172
tag utterance, 69–71, 75
adult-child conversation, topics and domains of, 82–9, 93–102, 180–2, 248–51

domains classified, 90–1
topics classified, 91–3

Bandura, A. & Walters R. H., 156
Bruner, J. S., 29, 115

Cazden, C. B., 212
child development, aspirations and goals of, 4–7, 12, 190–1
class factors in, 7–10, 193, 201–4
interaction with adults in, 7, 10–11, 28, 45
theories of, 2–4
Contact, 29, 103, 207
Coram, Thomas, Research Unit, 3
Cranstoun, Y., 29–30, 34, 162–3, 168–9, 197–8, 209
Crowe, B., 160

Dewey, J., 128

Education: a Framework for Expansion, 1
Erikson, E., 128

Freud, S., 128
Freyburg, J. T., 159–60
Froebel, F., 106, 128

Hartmaan, E. & Haarvind, H., 203

Isaacs, S., 81, 106

Karnes, M. B., 10

de Lissa, 128
Luria, A. R. & Yudovich, F., 115

McMahon, L., 29, 32, 209
Malinowski, 68
Marshall, H. R. & Hahn, S. C., 159

Montessori, M., 10

Neill St J. & Denham, E., 196

Oxford Preschool Research Group
    (OPRG), 4, 16, 29, 209, 211

Piget, J., 2, 128
Pre-School Playgroups Association
    (PPA), 29, 33, 103, 207
preschool, changing practitioners'
    attitudes in, 162–3, 169–89,
    199
  children in, 200–9
  physical structure of, 26–7, 41,
    197
  'teaching' in, 103–4
    practical guidelines for, 122–5
    styles of, 105–22
  research into, 200
preschool intervention, Educational
    Priority Areas (in UK), 3, 8
  Head Start (in US), 3, 8
preschools, and the State, 1, 2, 33,
    195–6, 206–7
  in Berkshire, 211
  in Nottinghamshire, 1–2
  in Oxfordshire, 1, 4, 32, 127, 129
  in Northern Ireland, 9–10
  in Miami, Florida, 4

research, implications of this
    project, 191–2

methods of this project, xi–xii,
    3–4, 15–18, 22, 26–7, 29–30,
    32–3, 34, 206–9, 228–247
  shortcomings of this project,
    196–7
Rutter, M., 8

Scaife, M. & Bruner, J. S., 84
Schaffer, H. R., 84
Smilansky, S., 159
Smith, P. K., 8, 194, 196
Snow, C. E., 98
Snow, C. E. & Ferguson, C. A., 28,
    54, 85
Sylva, K., Roy, C. & Painter, M., 4,
    11, 16, 16n, 92, 111, 114, 127,
    130, 158, 160, 193, 194

Tizard, J. & B., 3, 8, 40, 53, 82,
    200–1, 202–3
Tough, J., 3, 82
Turner, I. F., 5–6, 9–10, 103, 188,
    201, 203

Vygotsky, L. S., 56

Wells, C. G., 9
Weikart, D., 8
Wood, D., Bruner, J. S. & Ross,
    G., 115
Wood, D. J., Wood, H. A. &
    Middleton, D., 113, 205
Wright & Nuthall, 205